Advance comments on
Listening to Your Inner Guide...

"Perhaps there's nothing more important in this world than learning to listen to the inner voice to guide us. *Listening to Your Inner Guide* is a wonderfully clear new book that helps us greatly in this direction."
     — GERALD G. JAMPOLSKY, M.D., author of *Love Is Letting Go of Fear*

"*Listening to Your Inner Guide* will help you create the love you want in your life."
     — KEN KEYES, JR., author for *Handbook to Higher Consciousness*

"Jon Mundy offers the precious gift of bringing the noble principles of *A Course in Miracles* into heartfelt, practical application. I am deeply touched and inspired by the integrity of this work, I know that many will be blessed by this magnificent new offering."
     — ALLEN COHEN, author of bestselling
     The Dragon Doesn't Live Here Any More and many other books

"Read Jon's book quietly, thoughtfully, blissfully. But most importantly — listen to your Inner Guide as you do. I support Jon and his work wholeheartedly.
     — DR. WAYNE W. DYER, author of *Your Sacred Self*

Listening to
Your Inner Guide

~

Listening to
Your Inner Guide

~

JON MUNDY

CROSSROAD • NEW YORK

1995

The Crossroad Publishing Company
370 Lexington Avenue, New York, NY 10017

Copyright © 1995 by Jon Mundy

Printed in the United States of America

Library of Congress Cataloging-in-Publication Data

Mundy, Jon.
    Listening to your inner guide / Jon Mundy.
       p.   cm.
    Includes bibliographical references.
    ISBN 0-8245-1498-X (pbk.)
    1. Spiritual life.   2. Holy Spirit.   3. Course in miracles.
I. Title.
BL624.M854   1995
299'.93—dc20   95-13750
                                                      CIP

*To My
Darling Dolores*

All that is given you is for release;
the sight, the vision
and the inner guide
will all lead you out of hell
with those you love beside you,
and the universe with them.

— A Course in Miracles, T-31.VII.7

Contents

~

Part IV
OUR LAST REMAINING FREEDOM

Part V
THE ANSWER TO PRAYER

Acknowledgments

~

Thanks first to Diane Berke, my partner in the foundation and development of Interfaith Fellowship and *On Course* magazine, for her ever-present love and devotion, her constructive comments, and her suggestions for appropriate development

Thank you to Ruth Murphy. Ruth has been my principal assistant for the past five years. Ruth knows more about the running of our office than I do, and I am deeply grateful for her presence in my life.

Thank you to Meribeth Seaman. Meribeth has done all the paste-up and mechanical work on *On Course* for the last four years. She has also applied her excellent proofreading skills to most of the chapters in this book.

Thank you to Sara Emrie Brown for her friendship and for her editing of this book. This is the second book that Sara has edited for me and I am deeply appreciative of her always appropriate insights and observations.

Thank you to the members of Interfaith Fellowship, our church in New York City with whom I first shared many of these ideas. Interfaith has been a comfortable home of companionship and ongoing communion.

Thank you to the readers of *On Course* magazine who first read most of these chapters as they were published in *On Course*.

Thank you to Michael Leach, publisher and editor at Crossroad, for his encouraging words, his detailed reading of each chapter, and his suggestions for improvement.

Finally, my thanks to Dr. Kenneth Wapnick for his friendship of more than twenty years, for his devotion to *A Course in Miracles*, for having consistently fostered my own growth and understanding of the Course, for his reading of this text, and for his suggestions for changes and improvement. I have not, however, incorporated all of Ken's suggestions and I am sure he would not be in agreement with everything the reader finds in this book.

Preface

~

In the postscript to my last book, *Awaken to Your Own Call*, I raised the question, What's missing? What was missing, I said, was a more detailed description of the important role the Holy Spirit plays in *A Course in Miracles* and in our lives.

Awaken to Your Own Call was a comprehensive introduction to *A Course in Miracles*. Although reading *Awaken to Your Own Call* first would provide a more complete picture, this current work stands on its own and can be read without having read *Awaken to Your Own Call*.

The first edition of *A Course in Miracles* was published in 1976. The second edition, with minor corrections and revisions along with the numbering of paragraphs and sentences, was published in 1992. Over one million copies of the Course are in existence. References to *A Course in Miracles* in this work are from the second edition. The abbreviation "T" refers to the Text, "W" to the Workbook, "M" to the Manual for Teachers, "C" to the Clarification of Terms (found at the end of the Manual), and "S" to the Song of Prayer (a pamphlet from the same source as the Course). Numbers of parts, sections, subsections, chapters, lessons, questions, paragraphs, and sentences are provided as appropriate.

The ideas represented herein are the personal interpretation and understanding of the author and are not endorsed by the copyright holder for *A Course in Miracles*. Portions from *A Course in Miracles* ® © 1975 are reprinted by permission of the Foundation for Inner Peace, Inc., P.O. Box 1104, Glen Ellen, CA 95442.

A Course in Miracles may be purchased from the Foundation for Inner Peace. The single volume softcover edition is $25. The hardcover edition is $30.

Part I

Introduction

Chapter 1

The Call to Joy

❦

There is guidance for each of us,
and by lowly listening we shall hear the right words.

— Ralph Waldo Emerson

It is my intention to convince you (in case you're not already convinced) that for each of us there is an inner guide. Deep down inside there is a You that is very wise, who knows your every need and can answer your deepest heart's desire. This guide knows exactly the right decision you need to make, in each and every instance. When you listen to and let Him direct your every decision, life works out miraculously.

Most of us lead active lives with many responsibilities. Involved as we are in the world, inner life is neglected — sometimes almost completely forgotten. Most of us have not been educated with an awareness of inner life; instead we follow rules and regulations that have been given to us. Or we follow what we call our conscience, which may or may not have anything to do with inner guidance. Listening to our inner guide is a matter of reeducation, of paying attention once again to a valuable source of direction that has always been present for us though we may have forgotten it almost entirely.

Modern brain research suggests that the more we exercise our brains the longer we are able to put off senility. In a similar way, learning to listen to our inner guide takes practice and forbearance, but as with any exercise, the more you do it, the easier it gets.

The Tiny Mad Idea

The idea that there is in each of us an inner guide, an intelligent principle, an inner genius, an indwelling spirit, a little spark, a counselor, comforter, healer, mediator, and teacher is not new. The idea is as old as humankind. *A Course in Miracles* says that this Voice was placed in our minds at the very instant we decided to split off from the mind of God. The event

15

is understood mythologically in terms of what happened in the Garden of Eden. At some point man, woman, you, me, us — we decided it was possible to think a thought that was outside of the mind of God, and we have been trying to think that thought ever since.

> *Into eternity, where all is one,*
> *there crept a tiny, mad idea,*
> *at which the Son of God remembered not to laugh.*
>
> — T-27.VIII.87.6:2

The "tiny, mad idea" is that it is actually possible to listen to some voice that is not the Voice of God. For the past several million years, several billion of us have been listening to a crazy voice that tells us preposterous things. It tells us that we are separate; that it is not possible to get home again; that we are weak and frail and limited to bodies that are going to suffer and die and that is all there is to it. But that is not all there is to it. The memory of God still lurks in the back of the mind. Though often very hidden, God has never left us and we can remember Him at any time. We have all been in touch with our inner guide. When was the last time you heard His Voice?

- Were you a child and somewhat more innocent than you are now, and more interested in fantasy, fairy tales, stories, and other mysterious things that you do not now admit into consciousness? Were all sorts of things possible that are no longer possible? Were dolls alive? Did fairies exist? Were angels an easy possibility? Were there all sorts of other worlds, the world of the ants, the world of the leprechauns, other worlds in outer space?

- Perhaps you were reading an inspirational work and one line stood out with such impeccable, immaculate, and irreproachable truth you knew it had to be true.

- Maybe you experienced a moment of great synchronicity, some moment when there was a coincidence of events that were very meaningfully related.

- It might have come in a dream, intuition, or gut feeling.

- It might have come one day when you were standing looking at a field, a sunset or sunrise. Maybe you were just staring at a parking lot or some buildings, or maybe just looking at the floor.

- It might have happened because your old methodologies no longer worked.

- It might have happened because you are not very good at paying attention, and you got hit so hard in the face with what we call reality that you *had to* pay attention.

- It might have happened simply because you saw that you had been thinking about things in the wrong way and were in need of another way of seeing.

- It might have come in the voice of a friend or teacher who told you something you very much needed to hear.

- Maybe you head the Voice during a long walk, a drive in the country, while fishing or bicycling, or sometime when you were very relaxed.

I'm going to make a wild guess and say that 99.9 percent of the time we do not listen to inner guidance. Fortunately, there remains that .1 percent of the time when it can break through, perhaps with remarkable clarity. A miracle is seeing things as God does. It is the intention of this work to see things as God does, to get that percentage up, so that following inner guidance is a more frequent experience and does not occur once in a great while or come only because we have been lambasted with reality.

What Is *A Course in Miracles?*

The inner guide is described in *A Course in Miracles* as the Holy Spirit. *A Course in Miracles* is a self-study program of spiritual psychotherapy designed to help us remember God. We remember God as we undo our guilt through forgiveness. Although the Course is set in a Christian context, it deals with universal spiritual themes. There are thousands of spiritual paths (M-1.4:2); the Course itself represents *just one way* of reaching Heaven. The focus of the Course is on the healing of relationships. As it says in the introduction:

> *This course does not aim at teaching the meaning of love,*
> *for that is beyond what can be taught.*
> *It does aim, however, at removing the blocks*
> *to the awareness of love's presence.*

The Course consists of three books: a textbook, a workbook, and a manual for teachers.

- *The Textbook,* of some 669 pages, describes the theory of the Course.

- *The Workbook* consists of 365 meditative exercises, one each day for at least a year. You can spend several days on one exercise but should not try to do more than one exercise a day.

- *The Manual for Teachers* is 92 pages. It provides a clarification of terms and addresses some often-asked questions, such as: "How will the world end?" and "Is Reincarnation so?"

- A Notation of C meaning Clarification of Terms, is found at the end of the *Manual for Teachers.*

- *The Song of Prayer: Prayer, Forgiveness, Healing,* a pamphlet of 20 pages, from the same source as the Course was first printed in 1978.

Its Origin

The Course began in 1965 with Dr. Helen Schucman and Dr. William Thetford, both professors of medical psychology at Columbia University's College of Physicians and Surgeons in New York City. Frustrated with the competitiveness and backbiting that so often characterize academic departments, Bill uncharacteristically turned to Helen one day and said, "There has to be another way." Just as uncharacteristically, Helen responded, "You're right — and I'll help you find it." In this ground of joining in common purpose to heal their relationship, the seeds for the Course found fertile soil and took root.

No doubt a genius, with a well-trained and rigorous analytic mind, Helen was also very intuitive and sensitive to her dreams and receptive to visionary and mystical experiences. She also had a keen ability to tune in to the needs of others. Helen's Jewish father described himself as an atheist. Helen's mother was for a time interested in Christian Science as well as a number of other approaches to spiritual life. She was also influenced by a Catholic nanny and a black Baptist housekeeper, both of whom introduced her to their religious traditions. Though attracted to the Catholic Church, Helen followed no particular religious path.

Shortly after turning to Bill and telling him she would help find another way, Helen began hearing a Voice that she described as a kind of inner dictation, telling her to sit down and write. Being a rationalistic psychologist she feared she was going crazy. One day the Voice became particularly bothersome, and she called Bill to ask his advice. He suggested that it would not hurt to sit down and write and see what happened. And so began *A Course in Miracles*...

The Course was published privately in 1976 by the Foundation for Inner Peace. Ken Wilbur, who has spent many years studying the world's greatest spiritual literature, has said of *A Course in Miracles* that "it is on par with anything that has ever hit this planet." It is an extraordinary statement from someone who knows the world spiritual tradition as well as Ken Wilbur. This spiritual teaching has sold more than one million copies and is being translated into numerous languages. It is amazing to think that it has probably barely begun to have its impact. Thousands of study groups have sprung up around the world, and conferences on the Course are now held throughout English-speaking countries.

The Course is exciting because it works. It facilitates a positive change in perception enabling people to move from a fearful view of the world to looking at the world through eyes of loving forgiveness. Hundreds of thousands of people from all walks of life have found the Course meaningful.

The Voice of the Course

The Voice in the Course is Jesus. This is sometimes difficult to hear. If you believe that inspiration is something that happened, once and for all, a couple of thousand years ago or more and that is it, then you may not think this is possible. Yet it is clear that the Voice in the Course is Jesus. The author of the Course makes several references to his life as the historical Jesus of Nazareth.

One may also ask, who is Jesus? Do we mean a historical figure who walked upon this earth and taught a group of followers some two thousand years ago? Yes, but is that all? From the standpoint of the Course, to talk about Jesus is to talk about something timeless, beyond the world of birth and death. To speak of Jesus is to speak of the Christ, the Son of God, the Self that God created. To speak of the Self is also to speak of one's own true Self, which always has been and will be a part of God.

This book is entitled *Listening to Your Inner Guide* in keeping with the teaching of the Course that as we begin to awaken to the deeper call from within we discover our true Self, which is part of Christ. As we listen to the call from within, we will be listening to ourselves. "It is your voice to which you listen as He speaks to you" (W-pI.125.8:1). Our task then is to get in touch with the Christ, who is our true Self, by learning to ask for and follow the instruction of the Holy Spirit, Who is our Internal Guide.

My Journey to the Course

My introduction to *A Course in Miracles* was foreshadowed by my experience as a farm boy in Missouri. There I was taken with a sense of nature mysticism that whet my appetite for religious experience. At the age of eighteen I began serving as a pastor of three rural Missouri churches (1961–64). During those same years, while in college, I made frequent retreats to a Trappist monastery near Dubuque, Iowa. During my time in seminary (1964–67), I became progressively fascinated with the study of world religions. When I was twenty-seven, I spent the month of August at a Yoga Ashram in Canada, where, to my own surprise, I participated in a firewalking ceremony.

This firewalking experience so deepened my interest in Yoga and Hinduism that in the summer of 1971 I took a backpacking trip through India, spending time with Sai Baba, Rajneesh, and Muktananda. My last visit was with Muktananda. After several days in his ashram, I went into an underground cave to meditate. The cave, which was several feet underground, had no light and no sound. I sat down and said: "Am I supposed to stay here?" I had no more than asked that question when I thought I heard a "No," followed by a rush of thoughts, all of which said, "Go back to New York. There you will find what you are looking for."

Back in the United States, I resumed an active career as a Methodist minister and professor at the New School for Social Research and New York University. At NYU I met Judith Skutch, who was teaching parapsychology there. Judy was active in the parapsychology community in New York City in the 1970s, and she would frequently have friends over to meet Uri Geller or to see the latest in Kirlian photography or to discuss other interesting developments.

In 1974 I wrote a letter that was published in the newsletter of the Association for Transpersonal Psychology. At the time I was working on a dissertation on the relationship between psychotherapy and spirituality, and my letter expressed interest in any relevant articles, books, or information from the transpersonal community. In January 1975 Dr. Bill Thetford saw my letter, and he and Dr. Kenneth Wapnick suggested to Helen that it was a call for her to complete scripting the pamphlet *Psycho-*

therapy: Purpose, Process and Practice. She had started the work earlier but had never finished it.

Helen and Bill had heard me lecture a few years earlier at a Spiritual Frontiers Fellowship conference in the South. Helen remembered me and agreed that this was a call to complete the pamphlet. Helen completed the pamphlet in March 1975 and called to say that she had something she thought I would find helpful.

Helen invited me to meet her at Ken's apartment the following Sunday evening. At that time Ken was living in a small studio apartment on East 17th Street in New York City. I went to this meeting not really knowing what it was about. When I got there I met Helen, Bill, and Ken. Helen proceeded to tell me about *A Course in Miracles*, its development and its effect on those in the room. By this time, I had explored many different philosophies. Most of them had left me wanting something more. Though impressed by my colleagues, I was concerned that I would again be left wanting. At the end of our meeting it was decided that Ken and I would get together for further conversations. I walked home that evening feeling that probably the most important thing that had ever happened to me had just happened, but I was not sure what it was.

Six weeks later, in May 1975, Helen met Judy Skutch. Judy and her husband, Bob Skutch, together with Helen, Bill, and Ken, were to start the Foundation for Inner Peace, which became the publishers for the Course. Judy began by having three hundred photocopies of the Course made and distributed, so a small group of us got an early start in studying the Course. The Course itself was printed and released in July 1976.

It was not until July 1976 that I really began to take the Course seriously. Doing so was precipitated by an event that I call my death experience. A few days after the experience I wrote a detailed description entitled *Holy Hell*, which I read to Ken, Helen, and Judy at Judy's apartment on Central Park West in New York City. It was clear to me from this experience that: *we are not our bodies, we are making up our world, and this is not the real world.*

Ken and I became friends, and I sponsored a number of workshops with him as the leader (1977–84). Helen in turn became something of a mother figure, guide, mentor, teacher, and counselor in times of trouble — and it seemed I was frequently in trouble. I would meet Helen for counseling at Ken's apartment or at Judy's home, though never at her own apartment. She was always available by phone and was very supportive. She seemed to know intuitively when I was in trouble and would call to see how I was doing. Helen had an incredible ability to work with people in distress. At several points I felt frustrated with the Methodist Church and called saying: "I've had it, I'm quitting." Helen repeatedly said she felt it important that I not quit, at least not then.

Helen was very direct and would tell me what to do in very clear terms. I was not, however, a good student and often resisted her advise. At one point she said I should let go of a relationship to which I was quite attached. I could not see how I could follow her advice and find peace. In this case as in all others she was inevitably right. One of the most remarkable things about Helen was how she kept herself out of the spotlight when it came to the Course. Her name does not appear on the Course and she avoided public lectures on the Course. Helen died in February 1981. At her funeral, Ken gave an eloquent eulogy in which he discussed Helen's devotion to God, but he never mentioned *A Course in Miracles*.

The Church and the Course

My favorite PBS series is *The Ascent of Man* by Jacob Bronowski. I was particularly struck by the section on "The Starry Messenger," which discusses the life of Galileo. After Galileo invented the telescope, he was sure that he would be able to convince the world that Copernicus's theory was true, namely, that the sun and not the earth was the center of what was then the known universe. It was clear to Galileo that what he saw in the sky stood open and revealed. The results did not at all please the church. Galileo thought that all he had to do was show that Copernicus was right and everyone would listen. Dr. Bronowski points out how naive Galileo was about people in authority.

Once I began to understand the Course, I was sure it would be just a matter of time before it would revolutionize the church. For fourteen years (1975–89) I tried to introduce the church to the Course. During this same period of time, while I was increasingly working from the Course and continuing to study and teach courses on the various mystical traditions and Eastern religions, the church became increasingly conservative. The next thing I knew there were fundamentalists in my parish complaining that I was not preaching the "saving grace of the blood of our crucified Lord Jesus Christ." It was true. I was not preaching sacrificial blood.

In June 1989 I left the Methodist Church, and in September 1989 Rev. Diane Berke and I started Interfaith Fellowship in New York City and began publication of *On Course* magazine. Suddenly, a wholly new form of ministry became possible. Now through the 1990s, we've been able to actively and openly talk about the Course and watch its increasing popularity and acceptance.

I still believe that the Course will revolutionize the church by turning the focus from sin, guilt, and fear to love, forgiveness, and peace. I now realize that that change is going to come from lay seekers and clergy seekers alike who are rediscovering the heart of Christianity as expressed in the Course. *A Course in Miracles* may yet provide a Copernican revolution in Christianity because reality does not revolve around institutional systems of belief. It revolves around the truth.

A Course in Miracles is a philosophy of life that works for me as I know it does for hundreds of thousands of others. There are lots of ways of awakening. Still, there is but one mountain, one God, one peak experience. I may journey up the mountain from the west while you climb from the east. It makes no difference which side of the mountain we climb. We all begin from where we are. The more clearly each of us pursues our own unique path, the closer we get to the top and the more we realize how similar our paths have been.

Some Course Basics

The Course distinguishes two worlds, that of God and that of the ego: knowledge and perception, truth and illusion. Wrong-mindedness is the ego's way while right-mindedness is in alignment with the Holy Spirit. We are free to believe that our mind can be separated or split off from the Mind of God. A definition of the ego is that it is a wrong-minded attempt to perceive ourselves as we wish to be, rather than as we are (T-3.IV.2:3). We are also free to believe that our Mind can be returned to right-mindedness. Right-mindedness is the correction for wrong-mindedness and applies to the state of mind that induces accurate perception (T-3.IV.4:3).

The principles or "laws" that operate in the world of the ego are the laws of chaos, which rely on the belief in sin, guilt, fear, denial, and projection. The laws of God are the principles that express God's existence and the extension of God's Kingdom. These include the laws of forgiveness, healing, and freedom.

The purpose of the Course is to help us *remove the blocks to the awareness of love's presence.* These blocks are all the things that cause us to feel separated and afraid. Once we begin to remove these blocks, by looking at them for what they are and discovering that we do not need them, we become more open to right-minded thinking and more aware of our inner guide. The Course is designed to help us shift from hearing the ego's voice, which we listen to most of the time, to hearing the Holy Spirit's Voice of forgiveness.

Heaven is by definition a state of mind in which there is no dissension, discord, or division. The Course presents us with a monistic perspective. Traditional Christianity presents a dualistic perspective. According to traditional Christianity there is indeed a Heaven — but there is also a hell, a devil, guilt, fear, and the threat of eternal punishment. The moment we have a dualistic point of view we have a choice between good and evil, Heaven and hell. The ego by definition lives in a divided state. For this reason, we are never quite satisfied with things the way they are. We try to live our lives with a little bit of Heaven and a little bit of hell. We cannot, however, really have both, and creation, according to the Course, can know no opposition. Ultimately choosing for Heaven and our own happiness is the only decision we can make, so we might as well go ahead and make it now. If we continue to choose to live in a divided state we continue to choose to live in hell.

There is only one God, and there is ultimately only one way of living, namely, in accordance with the guidance of God. We are, however, stuck in the belief that it is actually possible to be separated from God. We think it is actually possible to think a thought outside of the Mind of God. We thus live within the fictitious dream world of the ego. According to the Course, this world is a dream, a fantasy, an illusion, a delusion or hallucination. Sometimes it may also seem like a nightmare.

The real world is Heaven. That is all that is really real. God and God's Kingdom are wholly true; the illusory world is wholly false. You can think of our predicament as that which we sometimes see in the cartoons where the cartoon character has a devil sitting on one shoulder whispering into his ear while an angel sits on the other shoulder offering some very different advice. Actually there is no ego (no devil); we're just caught for the moment in thinking that there is.

> *When the ego was made,*
> *God placed in the mind the call to joy.*
> *This call is so strange that the ego always dissolves at its sound.*
> *That is why you must choose to hear one of two voices within you.*
> *One you made yourself, and that one is not of God.*
> *But the other is given you by God,*
> *Who asks you only to listen to it.*
> **The Holy Spirit is in you in a very literal sense.**

His is the Voice that calls you back to where you were before
and will be again.
It is possible even in this world
to hear only that voice and no other.

— T-5.II.3:1–9; emphasis added

This book is about hearing His Voice and no other. It's about the joy that comes in doing His will and no other. It is the joyous discovery that His Voice is our Voice and we are all one with God.

I would like to turn first to share some early mystical moments. I suspect we've all had some of these same experiences. They were among our first intimations of immortality. Come with me on a journey of remembrance to a place called home. It is a place we've always been. It is the only place we can be completely healed and whole. Let us listen once again to a soft, gentle, comforting Voice calling from deep within, inviting us to dream a happy dream — a dream of awakening.

Chapter 2

Missouri Mysticism

~

Life not in Heaven is impossible
and what is not in Heaven is not anywhere.

—T-23.II.19:6

THE PARABLE OF THE MUSTARD SEED

And He said,
"With what can we compare the kingdom of God,
or what parable shall we use for it?
It is like a grain of mustard seed, which,
when sown upon the ground,
is the smallest of all the seeds on earth;
yet when it is sown it grows up
and becomes the greatest of all shrubs,
and puts forth large branches,
so that the birds of the air can make nests in its shade."
He told them another parable,
"The kingdom of Heaven is like leaven
which a woman took
and hid in three measures of meal, till it was all leavened."
All this Jesus said to the crowds in parables;
indeed he said nothing to them without a parable.
This was to fulfill what was spoken of the prophet:
"I will open my mouth in parables,
I will utter what has been hidden
since the foundation of the world."

— MATTHEW 13:30–35

As Jesus spoke in parables, so would I like to begin with a story that tells of something very familiar, yet hidden since the foundation of the world.

There are many things in life that we do not know and cannot know. Why is planet earth? Why space-time? Why human beings? Why consciousness? Why is there anything at all? We experience consciousness, existence, life. But why? What are we supposed to do here? How are we to live? Immanuel Kant once observed that there are two characteristics to these questions: (1) they are always there; (2) we cannot answer them.

While Kant may be right that we cannot provide concrete answers, it doesn't mean there are no answers. The first chapter of *A Course in Miracles* begins by talking about a kind of knowing called "revelation." "Revelation," the Course says, "is literally unspeakable because it is an experience of unspeakable love" (T-1.II.2:7).

How do we speak about the unspeakable? At best we can paint a picture or tell a story and hope the listener can see beyond the surface of things. The heart knows things to which the lips can never give utterance. The mystics say that their experiences are ineffable, indefinable, inexpressible. Many questions lack obvious and rational answers, yet answers may come by an awareness that has absolutely nothing to do with the accumulation of facts or what we call actualities. I would like to share one of the first ways I came to know things, a way I suspect many of us have come to knowledge or revelation, yet we may never have discussed it.

The Farm

Dr. Kenneth Wapnick says that his original mystical stirring came in listening to the works of Mozart. You might very well understand how that which first stirs within us could come through music. I was once surprised to find myself suddenly crying while listening to Chopin's *Polonaise*. But what first began to stir and move within me, what first began to pull me, came not while listening to music. It came through what I'll call nature mysticism. On a sunny day in the springtime you may be able to feel it. I expect we've all felt it.

I grew up on a farm in Missouri in the 1940s and 1950s, an only son with a younger sister. Our farm sat on top of a hill and was quite isolated by today's standards. Our front yard afforded a bucolic view of nothing but land, hills, and trees for miles. You could just see the smokestack of the electric plant in Mexico, Missouri some ten miles to the south.

As a boy I spent a great deal of time alone working in the fields, walking in the pastures, wandering in the woods. Weather permitting, I spent all my time outdoors, and most of that time I was working or playing with plants and animals. Like all farm boys I was expected to be available to do whatever work I could. Taking care of the farm animals required over an hour of chores each morning and an hour and a half or more each day after school. At one time or another we owned just about every kind of farm animal there is.

We always had horses, and for many years I rode a horse to the one-room schoolhouse where I was the only student in my class for eight years.

We had guinea hens and chickens, and there were always fresh eggs. One poor leghorn rooster used to annoy us with a wake-up call about four o'clock every morning till one morning we awoke to discover that Daddy had gotten up extra early and prepared leghorn rooster for breakfast.

I had a billy goat and my sister, Ann, had a nanny goat. We had big cheviot sheep with curly black hair (not wool), which was used in making women's coats. They birthed such large lambs that the lambs often had to be pulled out. Daddy would hold the sheep while Mother would do the pulling because her hands were smaller and she could reach inside. What a job! And what a sight for a young boy.

We had beef cattle and for many years a milk cow named Strawberry, who supplied our family with fresh milk, cream, which we separated from the milk, and butter, which we churned ourselves. There was usually enough milk left over for the many mouser cats that filled our barn. As I milked I would practice shooting milk into the cat's mouths. The cats would stand on their back legs and bat at the milk with their front paws. At one point I counted no less than eighteen cats. My father milked in the morning and on weekend evenings but it was my job each evening after school. We had little oinking pigs. We had cocker spaniels (Sandy and Knight) and collies (Lady and Butch).

All around were the animals of nature, birds of every description, snakes, turtles, possums, skunks, rabbits, and squirrels. Although I could not now bring myself to kill anything, I was, like all farm boys, an active hunter and fisher; rabbit, quail, ducks, fish, and other game were frequently on our table. Every spring there was new birth and, inevitably with so much birth, there was always the great mystery of death. It was all a wonderful enigma, an amazing riddle, a miraculous puzzle — and I wanted to know more about it.

We had a very large garden. In fact we had two of them and rotated between them each year, letting one lie fallow. We were, for all practical purposes, self-sufficient. The fence rows on the back of our farm were filled with blackberry bushes. Mother canned every summer, and our cellar was filled with green beans and canned tomatoes, pickled peaches and blackberry jelly. Mother put up fifty-two pints of blackberry jelly every summer, so once a week throughout the year there was a fresh pint of blackberry jelly on the kitchen table. We had a large strawberry patch. One summer we gathered fifty gallons of strawberries, which we sold for fifty cents a gallon. Gooseberry bushes surrounded our house and blackberry or gooseberry cobbler was a frequent dessert. As a 4-H project when I was sixteen I raised one hundred different kinds of vegetables (which included, of course, several kinds of tomatoes, corn, peppers, etc.).

All around our house there were lilac bushes. When I was very young I could climb up into the bushes and sit there inhaling their wonderful aroma. There were also cherry, plum, pear, and apple trees. As a child I would sometimes sit in the trees eating cherries or plums, spitting the pits out onto the ground around the tree until I was sick.

My choice to go into the ministry had nothing to do with some wise old preacher pulling me aside for a talk. It came not, as Jerry Falwell said it did for him, as a conversion experience at a Southern Baptist revival — though there were many Southern Baptist revival meetings in rural Missouri in the 1950s. It came not at the encouragement of my family or friends. I don't think my father ever quite knew how he came to have a son who was a minister. More than anything else, it was my walks in the fields and the woods. I kept feeling that there was something more, something calling to me, something invisible, something imponderable, something imperceptible, yet very real.

I stood and looked around at the cows grazing in the pasture behind the barn. I looked at one particular field. I looked at the meadows, the woods, the small lake and the pond. In the evening there was often a crimson sky stretching its colors out across the flatlands to the west — and at night how clear the stars in the vast, black sky.

Nature prodded, and so began the quest — the church, books, classes, professors, travels. But more than anything else I kept coming back to one particular pasture to take one more walk, to hear again some inaudible voice. Like a Moslem on a pilgrimage to Mecca, each year I have returned to that same pasture, usually in August. August holds the deepest feeling. August has all the music of nature — the bees, katydids, tree frogs, crickets and locusts. August has all the smells — the newly mown hay, the sun, the sweat, the dry earth, the energy of nature.

> *A province for the beautiful must be celebrated outdoors*
> *where there is no house and no housekeeper.*
>
> — HENRY DAVID THOREAU, *Walden Pond*

There was also the time alone in the woods. After school I would sometimes ride my horse to a clearing on the back of our farm that I called my Heavenly Spot. There I would lie on a grassy spot and watch the clouds passing over the branches of the trees high above. There too I would "disappear." I had there what I think the Course means by a holy instant. It was a space where I was completely safe, completely loved, and totally free.

Old Salt Creek ran though a corner of our farm in a wooded section we called the ten acres. We would go there to swim in a bend in the creek where the water was deepest, near a big tree we called Old Hollow. Old Hollow was the largest tree we knew of in any of the surrounding woods; it was completely hollow so that two or three of us could climb down inside it at the same time. One summer after I had moved to New York, I went back and recorded the sounds of that babbling brook and brought the tape back so I could listen to it at night as I fell asleep.

Walking the pastures, sitting in the woods, you can't help but notice something behind the obvious, something that itself causes everything to grow, to breathe — something that *animates.*

> *I went to the woods because I wished to live deliberately,*
> *to confront the essential facts of life*
> *and see if I could learn what it had to teach,*
> *and not, when I came to die,*
> *discover that I had not lived.*
>
> — Henry David Thoreau, *Walden Pond*

The Knowledge of Nature

Rudolf Steiner once said that when it comes to developing a taste for spiritual things, "one is very fortunate to be able to grow up within the context of nature." Here clearly in the daily events, in death and new life, a mystery unfolds and a story is told. With every new spring comes new hope, new joy, new sunshine and flowers; with every winter comes the ever-present reality of death.

To really know about the essence of things, the ancient alchemists said, watch nature. First, they said, it is necessary to know of the process by which things grow, ripen, rot, decay, and turn over into new growth. If you really want to know about the nature of God's Kingdom, said the alchemists, study the working of a compost heap.

From the alchemical point of view, the Kingdom of Heaven is *a happening*. We don't have the exact word for it in English, but the ancient Greeks called it *automate*. *Automate* means that which produces of itself." As a seed produces of itself, so the Kingdom of Heaven is in and of itself.

The Course says the creativity of God occurs as a process of extension. Extension is the ongoing process of creation, wherein spirit flows from itself.

> *In the creation, God extended Himself to His creations*
> *and imbued them with the same loving will to create.*
> *You have not only been fully created,*
> *but have also been created perfect.*
> *There is no emptiness in you.*
> *The Garden of Eden, or the pre-separated condition,*
> *was a state of mind in which nothing was needed.*
>
> —T-2.I.3:1

To succeed we need not force anything. We need only allow Spirit to flow from itself. The Kingdom of Heaven is something subtle and hidden. Jesus says it is inside us, working subtly like the rebirth of nature in springtime. Spirit is always stirring deep within — not in our bodies but in our minds. It's like leaven in bread. It is what changes everything. It grows we know not how, but with proper nurturance on this we can depend. It grows. Archeologists have found seeds thousands of years old that when planted come back to life again. God has planted deep within each of us the memory of Him. Though buried for thousands of years it can be brought back to life again. It just needs some light and nourishment. We just need to gently push aside the dark soil that has kept everything hidden.

> *To plant seeds, and watch the renewal of life,*
> *this is the commonest delight of the race*
> *the most satisfactory things that one can do.*
>
> — CHARLES WARNER

Creating by Sharing

Growth occurs at first as a process of inward turning — of becoming more and more concentrated — and then after the concentration there is expansion. Then there is a turning inward again and then another expansion. That's how things grow; it's like cells dividing. Pierre Teilhard de Chardin said that is the way all things grow, including our awareness.

> *Creating is the opposite of loss,*
> *as blessing is the opposite of sacrifice.*
> **Being must be extended.**
> *This is how it retains the knowledge of itself.*
> *Spirit yearns to share its being as its Creator did.*
> *Created by sharing, its will is to create.*
> *It does not wish to contain God, but wills to extend His being.*
>
> — T-7.IX.2:6; emphasis added

The most natural way for a thing to grow is logarithmically or exponentially. A chambered nautilus is a perfect example of exponential growth. It grows outward from the center with ever-increasing natural expansion of the previous dimension of its being. The outside of the shell grows as the organism focuses on inner growth. As we grow increasingly aware of our mission on earth and what we are supposed to be doing, as we focus increasingly on cultivating inner life, so does the exterior develop naturally, without distraction.

> *The earth produces of itself, first the blade*
> *then the ear, then the full grain in the ear.*
>
> — MARK 4:28

Jesus' parables tell us of the sureness of Heaven and the inevitability of its coming. First there needs to be a turning inward: first the grain, then the ear, then the full corn. The Course tells us that the extension of God's Being is Spirit's only function. Its fullness cannot be contained, any more than the fullness of its creation. "Fullness is extension" (T-7.IX.3:3). The full corn is the meaning of the grain and the ear. As we grow in awareness of our function on earth, as we begin to see and fulfill our function, we come also to know Heaven.

The parable of the mustard seed and the leaven suggest that the discovery of the Kingdom of Heaven is something subtle. There is something there but hidden. Deep inside the earth itself, deep inside our hearts, ourselves, somewhere there is an answer. Do you not know it? Have you not heard it?

Chapter 3

Remembering Self,
Remembering Home

❧

The world you seem to live in is not home to you.
And somewhere in your mind you know that this is true.

—W-pI.182.1:1

Every once in a while there comes into the mind some haunting memory of a truth that defies this world. A memory of Self, a memory of home keeps haunting us. Though called, we resist, distracted by our ego and our fascinations with the games and toys of the world.

Yet some try to put by their suffering
in games they play to occupy their time,
and keep their sadness from them.

—W-pI.182.2:2

Have You Not Felt This?

I used to spend time playing with antiques. I still have a passing interest in antiques, though I no longer actively buy or sell them. I used to go to antique shows and auctions and for a time had a share in an antique center. It was interesting, but I knew it was just an amusement, a distraction, a playing around with things. Sometimes I would look at the antique dealers and their fascination with whatever it was they were playing with and know that they too must know that this was just a diversion, a passing fancy.

Central to the Course and present in much of the history of world religion and philosophy is the idea that for each of us there are two selves. One of these is the true Self, who we really are. The other, the false self, is an illusion or a dream. One self we will call Spirit; the other we will call ego. According to the Course, Spirit is life. Spirit is our only true reality, which, being of God, is changeless and eternal.

Coming into the delimited framework of this world and ourselves as bodies only, we get caught in the little self, or ego. The ego is the belief in the reality of a separated (and therefore false) self that is made a substitute for the true Self that God created. The thought of separation gave rise to the ideas of sin, guilt, and fear and a thought system based on protection and attack.

If we live in the world of the ego only, if we think of ourselves as delineated by a body, if we have no awareness of the collective and our part in it, then life may seem like a 3-D horror with no exit. When suffering with some disease of the body or with some attachment or hang-up, it is hard to remember who we really are.

The man who is inseparate from all things
enjoys divinity as God himself enjoys it.

— MEISTER ECKHART

Before Jesus of Nazareth, the Greeks worshiped Christ as the *Logos, the word.* Logos means "inward thought." It also mean "outward expression." The author of the Gospel of John tells us that "first there was that which knew," that which grasped the nature of reality and formulated it into sound. "In the beginning was the word." Long before Jesus the Egyptians worshiped Christ as Horus. The Persians saw him in Mithras, the son of Ahur Mazda, the god of light. Mithras's birthday was at the end of December when the days once again became longer with increasing light. Every culture has believed in the perfection of the human being. We have always needed to see the perfect, to see beyond our limitations.

The idea of a true Self that is our inherent reality is described in Hinduism as Brahma-Atman. Brahma means God Atman means Self. Atman is inseparably connected with Brahman. Socrates' motto was "Know thyself," and the struggle to know oneself was a popular topic for Plato and Aristotle. The ancient Gnostics also took up the idea. It is an important concept in Buddhism and Taoism.

He who knows others is wise;
he who knows himself is enlightened.

— TAO TE CHING

Coming to an awareness of Self is an eternal idea because it is an eternal truth. The Self is our true identity as Sons of God.

Traditional Christianity can easily misinterpret someone like Shirley MacLaine standing on a beach saying, "I am God." It thinks that to say we are part of God means we are God, as though we have usurped the power of God. However, saying there is a true Self does not mean that we are God. God created us; we did not create God. To recognize ourselves as the being that we are means to recognize eternity. It does not, however, make us the creators of eternity. Jesus clearly perceived himself as this Self. He understood that he was God's Son. As he said it: "I and the Father are one."

The Vision of Christ

For traditional Christians, what Jesus did we cannot do; what he saw we cannot see; what he achieved we cannot achieve. Yet in the Gospels Jesus tells us that even greater things than he did we can do. Jesus in the Course describes himself as our elder brother. He has gone before us and blazed a trail we might follow. It is precisely because he has gone before us that we might follow. He shows us the way. "I am the vine. You are the branches." We are part of him. He is part of us. We are all part of the same Mind.

> *"No man comes unto the Father but by me"*
> *does not mean that I am in any way separate*
> *or different from you except in time,*
> *and time does not really exist.*
> *This statement is more meaningful in terms of a vertical*
> *rather than a horizontal axis.*
> *You stand below me and I stand below God.*
> *In the process of "rising up,"*
> *I am higher because without me the distance between God*
> *and man would be too great for you to encompass.*
> *I bridge the distance as an elder brother to you*
> *on the one hand, and as a Son of God on the other.*
>
> —T-1.II.4:1–5

Understanding ourselves as the Self means seeing things as He saw them. Beyond the darkness, and yet still within us, is the vision of Christ, "...who looks on all in light" (T-13.V.9:2). The vision of Christ, or the possibility of seeing what Jesus saw, is an ever-present and living reality for anyone who chooses to look upon the world without judgment, condemnation, and attachment.

Let me know myself Lord, and I shall know Thee.

— St. Augustine

To see as Christ sees, to share in his vision, is to see Christ in everyone and to let everyone see Christ in us. We see Christ in others by not projecting onto them, by letting them be. As we see beyond ego illusion to the Self in others, we know our own identity as this Self. This Jesus saw even from the cross. He saw clearly that his inheritance was the Kingdom of Heaven. He never doubted it. It is the center of his message.

When thou art rid of self (ego),
then art thou self-controlled,
and self-controlled art self-possessed,
and self-possessed possessed of God
and all that He has ever made.

— Meister Eckhart

Oh that we would but once learn to know ourselves!

— Jacob Boehme

Game Playing

Not knowing who we are, trapped in our little self, there are a million games we can play, any one of which may obsess us and take us over till it becomes the whole of life. There are men and women who devote all of their time to body building or to playing with comic books, baseball cards, or toy trains. Perhaps you're playing the corporate ladder game. Perhaps you're playing the Master game, the guru game, the holier than thou game. One game is not better than another. All games are distractions. They are the different ways we get caught in our specialness. They all take us away from Self.

I became a minister at an early age but could never get enthusiastic about being a churchman. I would go to the conference and district meetings. I realized that if I did not I was not going to get promoted in the church. Still I could not muster up enthusiasm for the corporation. Eventually I quit. To have stayed would have felt like selling out. As the Course says, "there is no one who does not feel that he is imprisoned in some way" (T-3.VI.11:1). My experience in the church is no doubt the experience of millions of others trying to play whatever game they are trying to play. Every school district, every police department, every social service agency, every hospital, every college, every office in the world is caught in one-upmanship and a pecking order that leaves people feeling frustrated. During the past couple of decades there has been an increased interest in entrepreneurship in the United States. We have an innate need to be able to make it on our own. Yet it's not easy or economically viable for many people to become entrepreneurs.

No matter what the fascination and distraction of this world — whether it is our good looks, our hobbies, or our bank accounts — still somewhere down inside we know it can't matter for much if our fascinations, distractions, and amusements keep us from an awareness of our Self. While we make a thousand homes, none content our restless minds (W-pI.182.3:3).

When Valueless Ideas Seem to Have Value

As long as we live by the pull of this world we never feel satisfied. The home we seek we cannot build in this world. We may find it, but we do not find it by the dictates of this world.

From the moment we are born, culture starts to work upon us, getting between us and God, foisting upon us cultural interpretations and perceptions. Blinders become habitual, and by the time we are adults we forget the blinders are there. There is a tendency to become unconscious, to forget Heaven, to live fascinated with our hobbies, our avocations, our family problems, our favorite soap opera, the church we attend or the club to which we belong. Doing so we forget about the blinders. Yet deep in our hearts we know: this is not it. We want to be at peace, and we know there must be something more. The call remains to wake up, remember Self, and come home again. We might even think it is literally our childhood home to which we would like to return. Yet as Thomas Wolfe said it: "You can't go home again." The Course says that "... the childhood of our body and its place of shelter are a memory now so distorted that we merely hold a picture of a past that never happened" (W-pI.182.4:2).

Still the child in each of us seeks our Father's house. In our truth we are all eternal children. We are all ultimately eternally innocent. Our innocence may seem so distant that we have nearly lost all memory of it. Yet the memory is still there, still affecting us. It is the child in us that our Father knows as His son or daughter and it is the child within us that remembers our Father. Still, it seems as though we would rather do anything other than remember our identity. Heaven is our natural inheritance, and we are free to refuse our inheritance. We have been given free will, and we can choose to focus on other things and ignore the Kingdom.

Are we forever then trapped in illusion? Is there no chance of awakening to Self and returning home, or do we get that chance only when we die? According to the Course we can remember who we are and return home in any moment. It comes, the Course says, with the simple realization: *I need do nothing*. Remembering who we are is not a matter of manipulation. It's not a matter of being good. It's not a matter of accumulating knowledge. All that is required is that we "be still an instant and go home."

We don't have to fight to become something. We don't have to climb any corporate ladders. We don't have to beat anybody to the top of the heap. When we are still an instant, when the world recedes from us, when valueless ideas cease to have value in our restless minds, then it is that we hear His Voice (W-pI.182.8:1).

Defenselessness Is Where Our Strength Abides

There is nothing to defend. Once there is nothing to defend there is nothing to attack. We can then let go of our making up of the world and just let things be. Once we can let things be everything is fine. There is nothing to do. There is no one to forgive or fight against.

A study done on children who were spanked found that they almost inevitably became parents who spanked their children. Why can we not hear the simple truth that as we give so do we receive? Forgiveness is a simple thing. It really comes in not creating a problem in the first place. It comes in not striking first ourselves. If the problem is already created then the solution comes in letting it go, in not compounding error. What if somebody did insult your ego? It really is not important. (Your ego, I mean.) Should we defend an illusion? It's forgetting who we're not and remembering who we are that brings freedom.

There is no need to get anyplace. Once we begin to pay attention to our inner guide, we find a Voice so poignant, so reassuring that there is no more fear. How can any of us fear our Heavenly Father? Once we pay attention to the call we see there is no need for shields, spears, and swords, no need for the illusions of this world.

Let's try a very simple practice: the practice of being still an instant. Once we are home where peace abides, once we know something of Heaven, we can reflect Heaven here, but we cannot reflect Heaven here if we remain caught in our little ego, believing in illusions, the toys and games of this world. We cannot reflect Heaven here when we believe the solution is to strike first. The solution comes in letting it all go.

Part II

Some Course Basics

Chapter 4

A Healed Mind Does Not Plan

~

A healed mind does not plan.
It carries out the plans that it receives
through listening to Wisdom that is not its own.
It waits
until it has been taught what should be done,
and then proceeds to do it.

—W-pI.135.11:1–3; emphasis added

The above quotation appears in Lesson 135 from the Workbook of *A Course in Miracles*; the lesson begins with the phrase "If I defend myself I am attacked." It then goes on to elaborate some of the ways we defend ourselves and why we seek to do it.

Most of us are so well defended, use defenses so unconsciously and frequently and with such ease, that we are not even aware of the fact that we are using them. *All defenses are ways of keeping the truth from being whole.* They are all ways for us to ignore our responsibility. Defenses give illusions full reality, thus making correction of our misperception doubly difficult. After all, if you defended yourself you must be right. Right? I mean you are right aren't you? Think about it. Once defended the defense is maintained. There is not one of us who has not defended ourselves unfairly, aware of the fact that we were acting unfairly, yet unable to stop the defense.

Defenses Do What They Would Defend

While we may *think* that defenses make us safe, they actually weaken our position. Defenses actually give us results opposite from what we intended. It is frightening to think that we must use defenses, lock our doors, buy insurance, learn judo, put extra money in the bank, take vitamins. All our defenses, indeed, all our plans, come from fear and reinforce the idea that we should be afraid. Defenses are frightening. They stem from fear, increasing fear as each defense is made. We think defenses offer safety, yet they speak of fear. The Course asks if it is not strange that — as we expand upon our plans and make our armor thicker and our locks tighter — we do not pause to ask what we defend and how and against what (W-pI.135.3:5).

Defenses take us down a never-ending road of increasing guilt: the guiltier we feel, the more we seek to defend. What would you defend? your body? a hurt ego? an upset mind? a disturbed thought or feeling? We never stop to think: What is being defended? Is this defense necessary?

In order to change things we need conscious awareness of what is going on. Without awareness of why we behave the way we do, we drift in an unconscious haze and life never gets better. In fact it gets worse. Read any good introductory text in psychology and you'll find the listing of ego defenses like sublimation, extroversion, workaholism, rationalization, emotional indifference, and apathy. While there are many forms of ego defenses, the most frequently used are *denial* and *projection.* That is, we either disallow and refuse to look at what needs our attention or we blame someone else for our own misperceptions and lack of responsibility.

There is not a one of us who does not know at the very moment that we are using one of our defenses that we are amiss, that something has gone wrong, that we are acting out of fear instead of love. The reason for our uneasiness is that we are trying to defend something that doesn't need defending. Now granted you're not going to walk down the street today without keeping your guard up. Jesus in the Gospels says we should be as wise as serpents and as gentle as doves. But the principle is literal: no defenses are needed. Even our body does not need defending. This does not mean that I would not automatically defend my body in the next second if I saw an attack coming my way — but the principle still applies. Jesus went to the cross to show us that the body was nothing. He also reassures us that we do not need to go to the cross just because he did.

An Exercise for Dropping Defenses

Any place where we drop a defense is a beginning.

1. Just begin.

2. The next time someone has a criticism of you in even the smallest way — stop.

3. Listen carefully. Do not defend yourself.

4. What is it they are saying?

5. Try to see what they are saying.

6. Now try to see what it is you have to learn from what is being said.

As the Course expresses it:

> ...*defenselessness is all that is required*
> *for the truth to dawn upon our minds with certainty.*

> —W-pI.135.21:3

It is in Workbook Lesson 135 that we come across that wonderful phrase, "A healed mind does not plan," with the very clear statement that our attempt to plan everything is a defense. It is a relief to know that we don't have to plan everything. Our self-initiated plans are defenses. We initiate plans because we think we need protection. When we initiate our plans we are trying to control the future, but the future is in God's hands. Miracles are merely the sign of our willingness to follow the Holy Spirit's plan (T-9.IV.:3).

If we are working on switching our allegiance from listening to the voice of the ego to listening to the Voice for God, then our task is to carry out the plans the Holy Spirit gives us. There is really nothing to figure out. There really is nothing to defend.

At this point we use our minds to understand the Mind. It is not complicated. We just have to use what the Course calls our "right mind." Using our ego-endowed minds has never given us what we really want, so the quicker we turn things over the happier we will be. Of course, the major problem of the ego is that it wants to be in charge. We do not want to turn things over.

The Authority Problem

We simply cannot believe that if we gave up and did what God wanted us to do, we would be happy. It looks like sacrifice, but sacrifice is not a sacrifice when we lose nothing and gain everything. Our real fear is not of pain or crucifixion; our real fear is of redemption or love.

One of the things that is fairly clear with children is that they, like all of us, are ego-bound. The difference between adults and children is that we learn to mask our egos so that we can demonstrate the appearance of genuine friendliness, generosity, and concern for others. We have all learned to keep our egos in check and not overdo our selfishness. It's called being civilized.

Children, though ego-bound, are less well defended. It's fairly easy to see that their egos are out of bounds. They are more rampantly selfish. It is also easy to see that the basic problem with children is the authority problem:

- They want to do whatever they want.

- They want to do it when they want to do it.

- They want to do it themselves.

- They want to do it their own way.

It should not surprise us that this type of behavior frequently runs counter to what parents, teachers, and other adults have in mind. Indeed we tend to think that if left to their own devices children would run amuck. Like little children, our basic problem is an authority problem. We simply are not willing to turn everything over to God, for it looks as though if we did, we would have none of our own will left. Yet we cannot be truly happy until our will is His will, that is, until we are carrying out plans that are not our own but those that have been given to us.

Our basic problem is that we say to God: "Thank you very much, but I would rather do it myself." And God says: "You have free will; you can do what you want. And in the mean time I will always be here if you want help."

When we work with God it may look like we are lucky, but there is no luck involved in doing God's Will. Miracles should not be under our conscious control. Consciously controlled miracles can be misguided (T-1.I.5:3) Our task is merely to surrender, to give in to the higher source that we are. When we get in touch with our destiny it's as though angels are pushing us from behind, doors start to open, and life feels free and wonderful.

There Is Nothing We Have to Do

A disturbed mind is indecisive, doubtful, and ambiguous. Is not your mind at peace when it is clear what you are to do and how you are to proceed? We enjoy being busy and having things to do. It gives us a feeling of accomplishment and provides a sense of order and direction. Of course, being busy is not always a sign of health. It can easily become a mechanism of denial and avoidance. Still, our minds are more at rest when there is a clear path to follow. We like to feel as though we are taking steps that are leading us somewhere. God has laid out a clear path that leads to His Kingdom. When we follow that path, when we are doing God's Will, things work out better and we are happier. We are here to heal and to be healed. The sooner we get on with doing what we came here to do the happier we can be. But having said that I must now add the following.

There is nothing in this world that we need to do. We don't have to write any books or build any bridges. We don't have to have kids or own our own home. Our first task is simply to get out of the way and let Him be the teacher. Lesson 155 says: "I will step back and let Him lead the way." We remove the blocks to an awareness of love's presence by giving up our defensiveness, including the defense called planning. We simply do not need to control, govern, direct, and manipulate every situation. All we have to do is to respond.

Even simple plans are defenses. The plan to go to the drug store to get medicine is a defense. The plan to go to the grocery store to get food is a defense. The Course is not saying don't go shopping or don't ever again make a plan. We can't meet someone at a specific place at a specific time without planning. We're not going to drop all of our planning. Unless, that is, we feel like being enlightened right away. If we want to drop everything and turn it all over to Jesus we could do that. Sometimes people do that but we usually awaken to our call more slowly.

Receiving Instead of Planning — Giving Instead of Organizing

In Lesson 135 we are asked to give fifteen minutes twice in one day to rest from senseless planning. We're not in a position to instantly give up all of our planning and turn everything over, so He breaks us in slowly. What is exciting about the Course is that it works and it is gentle. It enables us to move one step at a time. It's like giving up any addiction. You can go cold turkey, which sometimes works, or you can let go gradually. Letting go gradually, we do not get frightened by sudden change. We should not be afraid that we "will suddenly be hurled into reality" (T-16.VI.8:1). In my death experience I felt as though I was suddenly hurled into reality, and for that reason it was terrifying. The Course, however, helps us move one gentle step at a time so that our path seems smooth. It only gets bumpy when we try to go too fast.

We are simply being asked to receive instead of plan. Instead of trying to organize, direct, and manage everything and everybody we are simply being asked to love. *Love doesn't take any planning.* I've discovered in working with children that the main thing they want is simply for me to be present. All I have to do is be there and let the moment take care of itself. I don't even have to do any planning. The child usually has a plan for me. All I need to do, quite literally, is *play* along.

As we set our defenses aside, our true Self, the real Us, the real You that you always have been, automatically comes to the fore. When we set our defenses aside, what we are left with is love, and that's all we need. All you have to do with a child is to love that child. We do not need to figure out what the truth is. As a matter of fact, we will never be able to figure it out. Jesus is asking us to stop trying to figure out everything. He is asking us to stop organizing everything. Let him handle it for a while. Give instead of organizing (W-pI.135.22:2).

Whenever we are really focused on something, we know exactly what to do. In emergency situations we are sometimes forced to be very aware and very conscious. When we are very aware and very conscious there is no question about what to do; we just do what we understand we are supposed to do in the next second. In the same way, in the next second I can write another word, I can express another loving thought, or I can give my mind over to the Holy Spirit — or I can give it over to the ego and be fearful and doubtful about what I am to do, where I am to go, and who I am to talk to.

We once had a very disturbed young woman who worked for us. She was unsure of herself in every way and had a terrible time making decisions regarding even the smallest matter. Everything was problematic. Anyone she did not know was suspect, and all her problems were someone else's fault. She seemed to lack any form of inner guidance. With guidance there is no doubt about what to do next. You do next what is in front of you, whatever is asking for your attention, and you let Spirit help you make the decision you are going to make in the next second.

The Course is not asking us to never again make a plan. It's just asking us not to do it alone. The more we let go, the more we find out. There is someone who is willing to help. Someone else is there giving us some very sage advice. Externally life does not change when we let our inner guide take over. It just gets better where it already is.

> There is a way of living in the world that is not here,
> although it seems to be.

You do not change appearance, though you smile frequently.
Your forehead is serene; your eyes are quiet.

—W-pI.155.1:1–5

Following Spirit's plan simply enables us to be better at being who we already are. The Course tells us that we will awaken to our own call, for the call to awaken is within us. When He lives in us we are awake. The Course asks us not to set limits on what we believe the Holy Spirit can do for us (T-11.VI.9:4).

When you do what He asks you to do, you are more You than you have ever been before. You are who you are supposed to be. The difference now is that you are not doing everything by yourself — and you know it. If there are plans to make, we will be told of them. They may not be the plans we thought were needed, nor indeed the answers to the problems we thought confronted us (W-pI.135.23:2–3).

His Burden Is Light

The Holy Spirit does not have the same concerns we have. Children can get very upset and hurt over what we as adults regard as trivial matters. What other children think of them, for example, is a major concern. As we grow older we usually let go of many of our concerns about what others think of us, knowing that it may not have anything to do with what is true. In the same way, what we think of as major issues in our lives do not carry the same weight for the Holy Spirit, for He knows our problems are designed to keep our minds distracted. The Holy Spirit addresses our only real problem, the problem of separation. Overcoming separation undoes all lesser problems. If you're upset because someone insulted you remember that only your ego can be insulted and you are not your ego. The Holy Spirit is not upset at all and is concerned only with teaching us how to find the peace of God.

Jesus says his burden is light, his yoke is easy. It's easy because it's not important. The things we think are important mean nothing to Spirit. "Cast all your anxiety upon Him, because He cares for you" (1 Pet. 5:7). If we are doing what God would have us do with our lives, then we can relax and trust that God is going to take care of us. When we are doing the will of our Father, it is up to Him to take care of us. Heaven asks nothing. "It is hell that makes extravagant demands for sacrifice" (W-pI.135.24:4). Heaven asks for nothing but our doing of His will, but doing His will is nothing, for doing His will is doing our own will. It is what we want to do. There is no other possibility. Doing His will is our greatest happiness.

Let go. Go deeper. Let go of your concerns for this world. For just a moment, let it all go. Go deeper. Get good at letting go. Let Him work through your fingers. Your inner guide can guide your fingers across the keys on a typewriter better than you can. He is an excellent typist and does not make mistakes. It's true in all things, in playing a musical instrument, in anything: let go and let Him have His way with you. The experience is absolutely delightful, and there is no anxiety associated with it.

While we have been running about making plans that lead to death, God has laid out a plan that leads to life. All we have to do is follow it.

Chapter 5

Blocking Guidance

~

With the possible exception of someone who is enlightened, we're all crazy. People who say that they have overcome all limitation and are one with God are very likely to be considered crazy. Jesus said he was one with God and got hung on a cross. There is a similar story of a Persian mystic who, like Jesus, announced that he was the Son of God and like Jesus was also crucified.

This whole world as a place that is separate from God and His Kingdom came into existence (insofar as it exists) with the insane notion that it was actually possible to be separated from God. The Course says we should not underestimate the extent of this world's insanity. There is no area of our perception that insanity has not touched. Our illusory dreams are sacred to us, which is why God placed the Holy Spirit in us, where we placed the dream (T-14.1.2:6).

Here are a few examples of the world's insane ideas.

- The belief that we can get our way and be happy by making other people feel guilty.

- The belief that we are justified in withholding our forgiveness.

- The belief that we can find peace of mind if we become wealthy and famous.

- The belief that we can stop war by going to war.

- The belief that we can stop murder by murdering murderers.

The Course says that the logic of this world is totally insane — and leads to nothing. Insane people like Hitler have come to power, found justification for their insanity, and persuaded millions of others to go crazy along with them. To have an ego is to be insane. We are all insane insofar as we believe this world is real. We are all insane insofar as we choose to spend our time living in the past and future rather than choosing to live in Heaven right here and now.

We are all insane because we think we see something outside of ourselves while all we are seeing is a projection of our own fantasy. We are seeing what we make up. We forget we made it up and think we are seeing something independent of us. Nothing is out there. We see the world that we made but we do not see that we are the ones who created it. In our questioning of illusions, we should ask ourselves if it is sane to perceive what was as if it were now (T-13.VI.1:6).

During my graduate training in pastoral psychology we were required to spend some time working in a mental hospital. One day I was walking down the hall and noticed a woman holding on to the side of a door talking to herself. I went over close to her and she said: "I'm scared. I'm scared." She repeated the statement over again. A nurse told me she had been doing that for twenty years — living in the past, caught in guilt, fearful of the future, trapped in her own hell.

It Is Insane to Live in a World of Guilt

We hang on to guilt as though it were real, as though guilt defined who we are rather than looking at who we really are. Continuing to believe that guilt is real, we block awareness of inner guidance. "...Guilt is always totally insane and has no reason" (T-14.X.6:3). A woman in one of our workshops told us a story of how as a young Catholic girl she was required to go to her first confession but she could not think of anything to confess, so she made up a lie. She told the priest that she had told a lie. She then felt so guilty for lying to a priest that she never went back to church again.

While lying may seem natural, it is of course unnatural. "Miracles are natural. When they do not occur something has gone wrong" (T-1.I.6:1–2). True vision is the natural perception (T-3.III.4:1). Hiding from the truth, lying as a means of continuing to hide, blocks awareness of inner guidance. The problem is not that the Holy Spirit is absent. The Holy Spirit is very present. It is we who are absent, and we are unaware of the presence of the Holy Spirit to the degree to which we would seek to hide from God and ourselves.

Who among us has not or does not carry around a load of guilt, conscious or unconscious, that weighs upon us? Who among us has not engaged in denial and repression? Who among us has not felt jealous? Who among us has not projected our own irresponsibility onto others? We nurture each other spiritually by being aware enough of our own craziness that we do not judge others for their craziness but accept them along with all that egg that is so prominent on their beard or the bump on their nose or the cockeyed way they look at the world.

My cocker spaniel, Cinnamon, is completely blind in one eye, which is clouded over from glaucoma, and the head of my cat, Pepper, is permanently fixed on a forty-five-degree angle as the result of an inner ear infection that left him with this peculiar physical distortion. I was working at the computer and looked down to see the two of them sitting beside each other looking up at me — a one-eyed dog and a cock-headed cat. Regardless of their physical appearance I certainly love them. Regardless of their physical appearance they certainly love me. Regardless of the quirks and differences that exist among us, the Course asks us to accept each other as we are, as we would have ourselves accepted.

> *Let him be what he is*
> *and seek not to make of love an enemy.*
>
> —T-19.IV(D).13:7

What Do You Do about Being Crazy?

Obviously it's crazy to continue to be crazy. But we are addicted to craziness. We are obsessed by our guilt, and we want to hold tenaciously to it. It is impossible to escape from illusions unless we are willing to look at them. We cannot begin to give up an addiction until we are willing to admit that we are addicts. We cannot escape from our illusions unless we look at them.

We stay dumb, stupid, and insane as long as we think there is no escape from insanity. As long as we believe that this world and all its accouterments — the paraphernalia, the fluff and baubles, the soap opera of everyday life — are what constitutes reality, as long as we are unwilling to look at the truth, the insanity remains.

Mullah Narsurdin was down on his hands and knees looking for something in front of his house. His neighbor came by and said, "Mullah, what are you looking for?

He said, "I'm looking for my keys."

So his neighbor got down on the ground and began looking with him. After half an hour of searching the neighbor finally said, "Mullah, where did you lose your keys?"

"I lost them in the house," said the Mullah. "But there is more light out here." We cannot find what we are looking for if we are looking in the wrong place and continue to provide some crazy justification for looking for an answer where it is not.

With anything that this world has to offer, we are left wanting. Even when we get what we've been longing for, we soon discover that it does not bring us peace. I was watching *Life Styles of the Rich and Famous* with Robin Leach. He was interviewing a man who was worth hundreds of millions of dollars. He literally could buy anything he wanted. He had worked hard to get what he had and was now in his late sixties. Now all he could talk about was how afraid he was that he was going to die.

In order to get out of our insanity we have to give up addiction to insanity. We have to give up the thought that we have to be an addict, that we must live in a soap opera, and relinquish the illusion that there is no way out. There is a way out. Our inner guide knows the way and can show us where it is. On our own we do not know the way. We need help. Twelve Step programs work because of the willingness of the participant to say, "I don't know what to do — Help me!"

Fortunately, we don't have to do things on our own. Fortunately, there is a guide inside us that knows how to choose for sanity. The good news is that no matter how insane we may be, God's Will for us is Heaven and nothing can keep us from it. Our wildest misperceptions, our weird imaginings, and our blackest nightmares all mean nothing (T-13.XI.7:2).

Once we are awake, once we relinquish the past and allow for the present to come into our lives, there is no more guilt, no more insanity, no more separation from God. The Course is hard and easy. It looks hard because of the complex mess that seems to exist within the world of the ego. Yet the Course is very simple, for

- once we have made the decision to let it all go;

- once we decide that we cannot decide on our own and recognize that we need help;

- once we become receptive to that help, help comes!

If we really knew how beautiful Heaven is, if we really knew the peace that is possible, we would not want to hold on to a single shred of guilt, no matter how attractive that attachment might be. Peace is possible. Sanity is possible. It is possible to know the peace of God, but we have to be willing to give up our insanity. Of ourselves we know nothing — but with Him we can know everything.

Turn it over. Turn it over. Turn it over.

Chapter 6

The Dreaming of the World

～

There is a section in Lewis Carroll's book *Through the Looking-Glass* where Tweedledee comments to Alice that the Red King is dreaming about her and, were he to awaken, Alice would be *Nowhere* because she is only something in his dream. Tweedledee says that Alice would go out like a candle if the king were to awaken. When Alice complains that their loud talking may wake the king, Tweedledum counters, "Well, it's no use your talking about waking him when you are only one of the things in his dream. You know very well you're not real." Her frustration mounting, Alice insists, "I am real!" and begins to cry.

What is real? Is what we call our awakened world real or is it just another form of dreaming? Dreams are ego creations filled with ego symbols (T-6.IV.6:4). To study our dreams is to look at our own projections, our own fantasies and fears. We live in a constant world of dreams, not only our sleeping dreams but our daytime dreams as well, for we are perpetually making up the world.

> *What proof could you give if anyone should ask us now,*
> *at the present moment,*
> *whether we are asleep and our thoughts are a dream,*
> *or whether we are awake and talking to each other*
> *in a waking condition.*
>
> — SOCRATES IN PLATO's *Theatetus.*

The story is told of a Chinese philosopher who had a lucid dream in which he thought he was a butterfly. The dream was so vivid and real that upon awakening he could not but wonder whether he might now be a butterfly dreaming he was a man.

> *We are such stuff as dreams are made of,*
> *and our little life is rounded with a sleep.*
>
> — WILLIAM SHAKESPEARE, IN *The Tempest*

56

Dreams are a distortion of the world planned around the way we would prefer to see the world. Within the world of the dream all sorts of fanciful things are possible because we are making up the dream. In fact, the Course says that in our dreams we arrange everything (T-18.II.3:4).

The ego gives us nightmares and fearful dreams and continues to create fearful dreams during the day. It seems that the ego's world of sin, guilt, and fear is real and that the Kingdom of Heaven is a fantasy. At one point the Course says dreams are "perceptual temper tantrums" in which we scream "I want it thus!" (T-18.II.4:1). Dreams show us that we have the power to make a world as we would have it be, and while we are in the dream we do not doubt that it is real (T-18.II.5:1–2).

Each of us remembers enough of dreaming to recall that while we were in the dream we thought we really were doing exactly what we were doing in the dream. When we awake we say: "It was only a dream." We do not think it strange that the things we thought real at one moment at another moment mean nothing. Perhaps dying is rather like waking up. Perhaps we shall at that point turn to our companions and say: "I just had the strangest dream." It's interesting that no one ever has an ordinary dream. When anyone mentions dreaming they are very likely to say, "I had the strangest dream." The moment we wake up we realize that everything that seemed to happen in the dream did not happen at all. The Course thus asks us if it is not possible that we merely shift from one dream to another without really waking (T-10.I.2:4–6).

We walk about in a soap-operatic world filled with dreaming, toys, gamesmanship and a variety of ways to create and sustain illusion even in our so-called awakened state. The Course says that words are but symbols of symbols and thus twice removed from reality (M-21.1:9–10). With our increasing ability to create realities, is our new fascination with virtual reality just a symbol of the symbol of reality and thus yet another step away from reality?

> *All that we see or seem*
> *is but a dream within a dream.*
>
> — EDGAR ALLAN POE

Daydreaming

When we wake up in the morning we may think the dream is gone, but the dreamer is not gone and so the dream continues on. In our daydreams the constituents of reality seem different (we cannot, for example, fly in ordinary life while we can within the nighttime dream), but the world we normally experience is not much different from the world of our night dreams. By day and night we are still making up our world and filling it with illusions and delusions, anger, fear, fantasies, and anxieties. The Course goes so far as to say that all of our time is spent dreaming. Our sleeping and our waking dreams have different forms, and that is all (T-18.II.5:12).

The Bible says that a deep sleep fell upon Adam. Nowhere does it make any reference to his waking up. Ever since Adam and Eve, we've been trying to make our way in the world without knowing how. Lacking guidance, we've been making things up as we go along, and we've not been dreaming a very happy dream. Jesus begins his ministry with the call for us to awaken. The first word of his ministry was "repent," which can be interpreted, "Wake up!" When Buddha reached enlightenment he woke up.

Dreaming in Concert — Sharing the Illusion

Not only are we nighttime dreamers and daytime dreamers; as a society we also agree to dream a mutual dream.

> *In solitude we have our dreams to ourselves,*
> *and in company we agree to dream in concert.*
>
> — SAMUEL JOHNSON, IN *The Idler*

We dream our dreams in concert through television, magazines, newspapers, tabloids, gossip, rumors, lies, fantasies, and fears. There is a scene in the movie *Saturday Night Fever* where John Travolta's brother comes home to tell his parents he has given up the priesthood. In explaining himself to John Travolta, he says of their parents, "You can't really defend yourself against their fantasies. All I ever believed in was their image of me as a priest."

We may think we are caught in someone else's dream and find it hard for us to wake up, and we are fearful just like Alice in Wonderland. We need to assume responsibility for absolutely everything that seems to happen to us. As one of the lessons in the Workbook expresses it: "I am not a victim of the world I see" (W-pI.rI.57.1:1). Yet it may very well seem that we are part of someone else's dream. Children become frustrated thinking they must live within their parents' dreams, wives become frustrated thinking they must live out their husbands' career dreams, employees become frustrated thinking they must live out their employers' dreams.

> *No one can waken from a dream the world is dreaming for him.*
> *He becomes a part of someone else's dream.*
> *He cannot choose to waken from a dream he did not make.*
> *Helpless he stands,*
> *a victim to a dream conceived and cherished by a separate mind.*
>
> — T-27.VII.8:1–3

If we think we are victims of the world we see, we may very well feel as though we are part of someone else's dream. We need to accept responsibility for the way we see things — everything. There is nothing that happens to us, however much we might like to think it otherwise, that is not of our own choosing. The world is as we see it or as we dream it. As much as we may think we are caught in someone else's dream, each of us is responsible for our own dreaming. When seemingly bad things come our way, we can project and become angry and blame someone else, or we can see that it is part of our own dream — our own nightmare. We could see it differently. Jesus saw things differently. It's what made him Jesus; he did not get caught in the illusions of this world, and in his day as well as in ours there was much illusion.

Lucid Dreaming

A first step in changing things is to become lucid dreamers. The person credited with first using the term "lucid dream" is the Dutch psychiatrist Frederick Van Eeden, who used the term to describe dreams in which he was fast asleep yet had *full recollection and could act voluntarily.* Most recently we've seen accounts of lucid dreaming in Carlos Castaneda's works, where he reports being taught to achieve lucid dreaming by first looking for his hand in his dream in order to awaken his consciousness within the dream.

Though the Course does not use the word "lucid," it does ask us to become aware that we are dreaming while we are in the dream. This is true for both nighttime dreams and daytime dreams. We are to become aware that we are engaged in a constant process of dreaming. We are to become aware of our own part in making up the world.

All your time is spent dreaming.
Your sleeping and your waking dreams have different forms,
and that is all.

—T-18.II.5:11–12

Tibetan monks have for centuries cultivated lucid dreaming as a pre-requisite to seeking enlightenment. As a monk increases the frequency of lucid dreaming and develops the ability to modify his dream imagery by willing it to change, he gradually recognizes the illusory nature of the dream. This awareness then also enables the adept to recognize the waking world as illusory. A similar process is asked of Sufi initiates.

A person must control his thoughts in a dream.
The training of this alertness will produce great benefits.
Everyone should apply himself
to the attainment of the ability of such great value.

— Ibn El-Arabi (Spanish Sufi)

As we become aware of our dreams of both the nighttime and daytime variety, we can begin to change the dream, once the dreamer has been recognized.

God's teachers choose to look on dreams awhile.
It is a conscious choice.
For they have learned that all choices are made consciously,
with full awareness of their consequence.
The dream says otherwise,
but who would put his faith in dreams
once they are recognized for what they are?
Awareness of dreaming is the real function of God's teachers.
They watch the dream figures come and go,
shift and change, suffer and die.
Yet they are not deceived by what they see.

—M-12.6:2–11

The Happy Dream

From the standpoint of the Course we are to transfer our nightmares into happy dreams. First, we must recognize that we are dreaming. Once we

become aware that we are dreaming we are to turn our dreaming o
to the Holy Spirit, who can help us dream happy dreams. Happy dream
are still illusory. They are still dreams. Now, however, we begin to dream
of Heaven instead of hell. Now we begin to dream of release instead of
imprisonment. Happy dreams that the Holy Spirit brings are different from
the dreaming of the world, where we merely dream we are awake. Happy
dreams are heralds of the dawn of truth into the mind. "They lead from
sleep to gentle waking..." (W-pI.140.2:7). It is not difficult to change a
dream once the dreamer has been recognized.

> Rest in the Holy Spirit,
> and allow His gentle dreams to take the place
> of those you dreamed in terror and in fear of death.
> He brings forgiving dreams
> in which the choice is not who is the murderer
> and who shall be the victim.
> In the dreams He brings there is no murderer and there is no death.
> The dream of guilt is fading from your sight,
> although your eyes are closed.
> A smile has come to lighten up your sleeping face.
> The sleep is peaceful now, for these are happy dreams.
>
> —T-27.VII.14:2–7

Happy dreams are characterized by:

- appreciating the kindness of others instead of dwelling on their mistakes.

- thinking of others' thoughtfulness instead of counting up the hurts (T-27.VII.14:8).

- seeing others in perfect health and perfect freedom from all forms of deprivation and safe from disaster of all kinds (T-30.VIII.2:5).

- forgiving others and seeing not problems but solutions, not hurts but healing.

Forgiveness and the End of Dreaming

It is impossible to forgive someone else, for it is our own sins we see in
them. We want to see sin in others in order not to look at it in ourselves.

Forgiveness of another is an illusion. "Yet it is the only happy dream in all the world, the only one that does not lead to death" (S-2.I.4:1–5). Just as the Atonement is the only defense that does not lead to further defensiveness, so forgiveness is an illusion that does not lead to further illusion. Forgiveness is an illusion because there is nothing to forgive in the first place. There is only something to forgive if we think there is something to forgive. The truth is that there is nothing to forgive. It's just that we're dreaming it is so.

> *Illusions make Illusion. Except one.*
> *Forgiveness is illusion that is answer to the rest.*
>
> — W-pI.198.2:8–10

Forgiveness is the end of dreaming because it is a form of awakening. Forgiveness is not the truth, but it points to where the truth is. Forgiveness leads us out of disaster, not into further disaster. Ultimately, once we have forgiven we see that no forgiveness was necessary; we just thought there was. In the process of forgiving we discover who we really are. We awaken to our own call. We have found our way home again. Salvation is a happy dream in which we forgive all things that no one ever did, overlook what is not there, and not look upon the unreal as reality. The Course asks us to "...be free of all the dreams of what we never were and seek no more to substitute the strength of idle wishes for the Will of God" (T-30.IV.7:1–5).

> *Happy dreams come true,*
> *not because they are dreams,*
> *but only because they are happy.*
> *And so they must be loving.*
> *Their message is, "Thy will be done."*
> *and not, "I want it otherwise."*
>
> — T-18.V.4

The Holy Spirit can use all that we give to Him for our salvation. Thus can we also give him our dreams to let them be converted from nightmares to happy dreams. Things change when we begin to become more receptive to what the Holy Spirit can show us. He leads us into gentle, reassuring dreams.

Prophetic Dreams

The dreams the Holy Spirit brings will always be dreams of comfort; they will be peaceful dreams of reassurance. There are five dreams in the first two chapters of the Gospel of Matthew. Each of these dreams that come to Mary and Joseph and the Wisemen is a dream of reassurance; Joseph, for example, is told not to be afraid to take Mary as his wife.

I have a good friend whose father died. She was very close to her father and very upset over his death. A few days after his death she dreamed that the phone was ringing in the kitchen and she was struggling to get up. Finally, she got up and went to the phone and it was her father. He said he just wanted to tell her that he was fine and he loved her and her mother very much. She later realized that the whole thing was a dream. We probably all know of many similar examples.

> ... the Holy One, the Giver of the happy dreams of life,
> Translator of perception into truth,
> the holy Guide to Heaven given you,
> has dreamed for you this journey
> which you make and start today....
> Into Christ's Presence will we enter now,
> serenely unaware of everything
> except His shining face and perfect Love.

> —W-pI.157.8:2 and 9:1

Part III

The Voice for God

Chapter 7

The Experience of the Holy Spirit

~

If there is an idea that is universal to all religions, it is the idea of the Holy Spirit. While Jesus is worshiped as the central focus for Christians, Mohammed holds a place of special honor for Muslims, and the teachings of the Buddha are central to Buddhism, the Holy Spirit crosses all boundaries.

Varieties of Experience

Tribal religions have always believed in the presence of a spirit who was thought to inhabit all people. They observed people going into trance-like states induced by singing and dancing, high enthusiasm and fervor. They might tell us that their heads were in the clouds and they were talking to the Gods. Tribal religions share a strong belief in *animism*, the belief that all things are filled with spirit — animals, plants, even rocks and sacred places.

The **Zoroastrians** of ancient Persia more than three thousand years ago spoke of a Holy Spirit that they called the *Spenta Mainu*.

The **Stoics** of ancient Greece referred to the Holy Spirit as "an intelligence principle pervading the cosmos." Socrates and Plato also talked about the "inner genius" that brought light into one's soul.

In **Judaism,** the Divine Spirit is called the *Ruach* (Breath) *Hakodesh* (Holy). To it are attributed the strength of Samson and the wisdom of Solomon. Holy Spirit is also called *Shechinah* and is thought of as embodying the feminine, nurturing aspects of God as well as divine inspiration. It is considered the aspect of God that entered into the exile experience of humankind after the fall, the indwelling spark of the divine in human beings. In *A Course in Miracles* as well, the Holy Spirit comes into existence at the exact moment of the separation in order to serve as a bridge or a link back to God.

Throughout the **New Testament** the terms "Counselor," "Comforter," "Healer," "Guide," "Mediator," and "Teacher" are all used to reflect different qualities of the Holy Spirit. All of these same terms are also used in *A Course in Miracles*. **St. Paul**, in Corinthians, speaks of the Holy Spirit as the "indwelling Spirit."

In **Islam** the Holy Spirit is identified as the angel Gabriel who first spoke to the prophet Mohammed. We find this same Gabriel in the Old and New Testaments. It is Gabriel who tells Mary about the coming birth of Jesus. In a similar way an angel in the Course is not to be confused with a celestial being but is understood as an extension of the thought of God and thus a form of inner guidance. An angel is a messenger who brings a communication from God. The angels in the birth story of Jesus come to Mary in a dream. Joseph had an angel appear to him in a dream. The wise men had an angel appear to them in a dream. The ancients paid attention to their dreams, for they felt their dreams were communication that came to them when their ordinary mind was at rest.

Meister Eckhart, the great medieval mystic, spoke of the "little spark" that could enlighten one's way.

Henry David Thoreau, the New England Transcendentalist of the nineteenth century, said that the degree to which we are true to ourselves is the degree to which we pay attention to our own "inner genius."

Even in **the contemporary form** of the movie trilogy *Star Wars* by George Lukas we might think of "the Force" as an ever-present superior form of all-pervasive universal and benevolent knowledge that knows and directs all things.

Author and *Course in Miracles* student Robert Perry refers to the Holy Spirit as "the Perfect Parent." What do perfect parents do? Perfect parents know the appropriate loving response. They always know how to direct their children. If the function of the Holy Spirit is to interpret God's Will for us in our lives and if God is our Father then certainly the Holy Spirit fulfills the function of Father in this regard. The Holy Spirit differs from an earthly father in that His advice is not external to us but internal.

A Course in Miracles makes direct mention of the Holy Spirit no less than 758 times, and there are many more times that the Holy Spirit is referred to indirectly. The Holy Spirit is referred to in the Course as:

Our inner Guide — God's Answer to separation — The Communication Link between God and His separated Sons — The memory of God and His Son — The One Who sees our illusions — The Voice for God — The Bridge — The Comforter — The Mediator — The Teacher — The Translator

The Course also says:

> *The Holy Spirit is the only part of the Holy Trinity*
> *that has a symbolic function.*

> —T-5.I.4:1

> *The Holy Spirit is the Christ Mind*
> *which is aware of the knowledge that lies beyond perception.*
> *He came into being with the separation as a protection,*
> *inspiring the Atonement principle at the same time.*

> —T-5.I.5:2

The Atonement principle is the principle by which all this mess that we have gotten ourselves into will be undone. Hearing the Voice of the Holy Spirit begins to happen as we lay our egos aside. As the inspirer of the Atonement principle, the Holy Spirit has the task of undoing what the ego has made.

> *The Holy Spirit is the idea of healing.*

> —T-5.III.2:1

> *The Holy Spirit is God's Answer to the ego.*

> —T-5.III.5:3

Symbols for the Holy Spirit

There are many symbols for the Holy Spirit, some more common than others. I'll briefly examine these symbols, beginning with the lesser known and moving to the more familiar. A symbol is only a symbol and not the thing itself. The Course repeatedly reminds us that we should not confuse form and content.

A Seal. Over time most of the saints have come to have their own symbol or seal. A seal has the quality of impressing, securing, and authenticating.

Oil. Oil has the property of healing, comforting, illuminating and consecrating. Healing oils were popular in Jesus' day. The anointing of Jesus with oil occurs more than once in the New Testament. Even today a massage with healing oils is thought to have a helpful healing, calming affect on one's body and soul.

Water. Water in the form of rain and dew represents cleansing, fertilizing, and refreshing, as water in the spring brings the earth back to life. It is a symbol of abundance, as water is freely given from the heavens to the earth. When Jesus is baptized with water by John the Baptist, the Holy Spirit descends upon him. Baptism is a holy act in many different religions, not just Christianity.

Fire. Fire purifies and illuminates. For tens of thousands of years fire (with its warming, cooking, purifying, energizing, and illuminating qualities) has been one of humankind's best friends. Much of religious ceremony originated around fire, with singing and the telling of stories.

The Zoroastrian centers of worship are known as fire temples, and a fire is kept burning in the center of the temple twenty-four hours a day. The ancient alchemists were fascinated with fire because it had the ability to amalgamate metal. Ancient potters and smithies who worked with fire were the grandfathers of the alchemists. Just as alchemy concerned itself with the transformation of something base into something golden, so the Holy Spirit helps to transform us from our base ego self into the true golden Self we were meant to be.

The Dove. A dove is the symbol of peace, gentility, meekness, innocence, and a forgiving heart. The dove is a universal symbol throughout all cultures that has fully retained its meaning throughout the centuries.

The three scenes in which the figure most frequently occurs in art are in representations of the annunciation to the Virgin, baptism of Jesus by John in the River Jordan, the creation of the world.

From early times, the Holy Spirit has been symbolized by the dove in Christian art. However, around the tenth century there arose the custom of representing the Holy Spirit in human form. Six hundred years later this practice was discontinued by Pope Urban VIII, who issued an edict prohibiting it. The dove was again established as a primary symbol.

Wind and Air.

> *The wind bloweth where it listeth,*
> *and you hear the sound thereof,*
> *but you cannot tell where it comes from and where it goes;*
> *so is everyone that is born in Spirit.*
>
> — JOHN 3:8

Quite literally the word "Spirit," from the Latin *spirare*, means: blowing, wind, breath, and air. Like the Holy Spirit, wind is independent, powerful, sensible in its effect, and reviving. There is a very literal sense in which from the moment one takes one's first breath one is "inspired." With the first breath we have life as an independent being in the world. From that moment until one's last breath, when one "expires," the body can function in the world.

Wind, like the Holy Spirit, is invisible. We see the trees bending in the wind, we feel the wind as it strikes our bodies, but we do not see the wind. For ages people have used the power of the wind to grind grain in mills and push sails across the oceans. The Holy Spirit is also, like air, omnipresent. We cannot see the invisible, but we can see its effects; therefore we know it must be there. By perceiving what it does, we recognize its being. We cannot see the Holy Spirit, but we can see His manifestations. His presence can become compellingly real to us as His presence becomes manifest through us (T-12.VIII.4:1).

A Voice. Closely associated with breath and wind is the voice. Like air, the voice — sound waves — is also invisible. We may think of the Holy Spirit as Dr. Carl Jung did, as the soft whisper of God in the human being. One of my favorite hero stories is *The Hymn of the Pearl.* When the hero got lost in the world, his parents noticed what had befallen him and wrote a letter calling him to awaken, rise out of sleep, become aware of his bondage and throw it off, and remember his origin. The letter came in the form of an eagle that "became wholly speech." At the sound of His Voice, the hero awoke, took up the letter, broke the seal, and recalled in his heart the purpose of his journey.

In the beginning of the Gospel of John we read that in the beginning was *the word* and the word was *with God.* It is the word that helps us unlock our dumb ego minds and enables us to know God who is beyond all words. We may hear the Holy Spirit speaking to us in quiet, simple ways. We may experience the Holy Spirit as quite literally speaking to us, as Gabriel spoke to Mohammed or Mary, or in more indirect and subtle ways.

We do not have to take this Voice literally. We do not have to think that we are going to hear an external voice saying: "Hey, Bill!" It probably will not come that way. That's not to say that that is an impossibility, but the Voice is more likely to be much more subtle.

When we ask for guidance it does not matter whom we call upon. Any name will do. A name is just a word. If you feel comfortable calling upon Jesus, then call upon Jesus. If you feel more comfortable calling upon the Holy Spirit, call upon the Holy Spirit. If you feel more comfortable calling upon Wana Tago, then call upon Wana Tago. The words do not matter. In every age and every culture there has been present for us the awareness that we are not alone and that there is a higher force or principle that can teach us if we are willing to be taught.

The Course makes repeated references to the "Holy Spirit," so that is the term I'm using, but what I'm talking about can be called by many different names. The inner guide is there. He has always been there. He has never left us. It is impossible that he should ever leave.

Chapter 8

The Holy Spirit in A Course in Miracles

~

I will pray to the Father,
and He will give you another Counselor to be with you forever.

And the Spirit of truth, whom the world cannot receive,
because it neither sees Him nor knows Him,
but you know Him, for He dwells with you and will be in you.

The Counselor, the Holy Spirit,
whom the Father will send in my name,
He will teach you all things,
and bring to your remembrance all that I have said to you.

— JOHN 14:16–17, 26

Nevertheless I tell you the truth;
it is to your advantage that I go away,
for if I do not go away,
the Counselor will not come to you;
but if I do I will send Him to you.

When the Spirit of truth comes,
He will guide you into all the truth;
for He will not speak on His own authority,
but whatever He hears He will speak,
and He will declare to you the things that are to come.

— JOHN 16:7, 13

The Holy Trinity

In terms of traditional Christianity and the Course we may think of God, Christ, and the Holy Spirit being one and the same in the Trinity yet having different functions:

73

God is the Father and Creator, the First Person in the Trinity, the Source of all being and life. Fatherhood is established by the existence of a child. God is the first Cause, His Son is His Effect. God's essence is Spirit, which is shared with all creation.

Christ is the Second Person of the Trinity, our true Self that includes our creations, the Self that God created by extension of His Spirit. Though Christ creates as does His Father, he is not the Father since God created Christ. Christ did not create God.

Jesus in the Course is the one who first completed his part in the Atonement. By transcending his ego, Jesus has become identified with Christ and now serves as our model for learning. It is his Voice we hear speaking to us in the Course. Jesus' will is God's Will and our decision to hear his Voice is the decision to hear the Voice for God (T-8.IV.3:9).

The Holy Spirit is the Third Person of the Trinity, metaphorically described in the Course as God's answer to separation. The Holy Spirit is the Voice for God that unites us with God.

(See Dr. Kenneth Wapnick's *Glossary-Index for A Course in Miracles*, Foundation for A Course in Miracles, 1993.)

In terms of their function as our inner guide, Jesus and the Holy Spirit are one and the same. They are not one and the same from a theological point of view. Since Jesus has transcended his ego and does not have an ego voice speaking within him, the only Voice that speaks through him is that of the Holy Spirit. Thus it is that he says he is the manifestation of God's Voice, i.e., the Holy Spirit.

God and the Holy Spirit

The Holy Spirit both recognizes the illusions of guilt and the fears that are in our mind. At the same time He remembers the truth of who we really are. From the standpoint of the Course, God the creator does not know about the content of our illusory dream. An analogy often used by Dr. Wapnick is to think of yourself as a parent looking in on your child at night, you see your child tossing and turning and you know that your child is having a dream, but you do not know what the dream is. As real as the dream is to the child, as soon as the child wakes up the dream is gone. God knows that we are asleep and we are dreaming, but God does not know the content of our dream. God sends the Holy Spirit from His mind into the Son's mind to awaken him to reality and show him that his dreams are not real.

The Holy Spirit is the part of God that extends into the ego mind to teach us that the ego mind is not real. The Holy Spirit comes into the dream world of our mind to give us a different message, namely, that we could make another choice, a choice for love instead of fear, a choice for truth instead of illusion.

When I was in seminary, I read a book titled *Spirit, Son and Father,* in which the author put forth the theory that we have so overidentified the Trinity with Father first, Son second, and Holy Spirit third that we forget that the Trinity is an equality, and if it is an equality then we could just as well say Spirit, Son, and Father as Father, Son, and Spirit. In terms of the Course, however, and most of traditional Christianity, God is the Creator, Christ is the creation of God, and the Holy Spirit is the link between the two.

Before he leaves his bodily presence, Jesus tells his disciples that there is One who will always be with them, namely, the Holy Spirit. No doubt the disciples were so enamored of Jesus, so overwhelmed by him and his presence in the world that it was hard for them to think that they could contact God on their own. Thus, Jesus tells them that it is to their advantage that he goes away, no doubt so they could become aware of their own inner guide.

The Holy Spirit Is the Christ Mind

Let this mind be in you, which was also in Christ Jesus.

— PHILIPPIANS 2:5

We can think of the Holy Spirit as the mind that came to full realization in Jesus and is available to us all as we are the Christ yet unrealized. The Holy Spirit is the Christ Mind that came into being with the separation and represents a state of mind close enough to One-mindedness that transfer to One-mindedness is possible through Him. The Holy Spirit thus induces a kind of perception in which many elements are like those in the Kingdom of Heaven.

The Holy Spirit is in us in a very literal sense, not in our bodies, which are ephemeral and will die, but in our minds, which are eternal and cannot die. This little devil that sits on our shoulder and whispers in our ear is a projection of the ego. However, in terms of the Course, neither the devil nor the ego really exists. They have no eternal reality. Neither the devil nor the ego is to be fought against, as that makes them real in our mind. Making the unreal real, we live within an illusion.

Between these two decisions (God or the ego) that seem to constantly present themselves to us there is ultimately only one right choice that any of us can make, and that is to decide for and with God. This is also the decision we wish to make for ourselves. This is the decision that is in line with our higher Self. Our inner guide is difficult to hear because the ego's voice is so loud, it so often shrieks with such terror and it is so distracting, that it makes it impossible to hear the Voice for God that is always quiet and subtle and always there. "It is a loud, obscuring voice whose shrieks would silence what the Holy Spirit says and keep His words from your awareness" (T-27.VI.1:2).

The Inspired Individual

Jesus instructed to his disciples:

> *When they deliver you up,*
> *do not be anxious how you are to speak or what you are to say;*
> *for what you are to say will be given to you in that hour;*
> *it is not you who speak;*
> *but the Spirit of your Father speaking through you.*

> — MATTHEW 10:19–20

Because that they had no formal instruction in speech, Jesus' disciples asked him how they were to preach. He told them not to worry, but simply to open their mouths and let the Spirit of God speak through them. Having willingly become disciples and having done what was necessary to be sensitive beings, receptive to the guide of Spirit, they were simply to relax and let that same Spirit work through them.

The greatest inspiration has always come to individuals. The greatest achievements in human history have taken place within the inspired hearts of men and women who were aware of the presence in their lives of something greater than just themselves. God through the Holy Spirit has spoken to individuals — to Abraham, Moses, Mohammed, Gautama Buddha, Jesus, or Helen Schucman. And He speaks to you and to me all the time, if we are but willing to listen. Individuals are inevitably ahead of institutions, for it is easier for an individual to be open to inspiration than for a whole community. As individuals, we can see things that collectively cannot be seen.

Think about when you have felt real joy in your life and I'd guess it was when you had an insight or inspiration, when some new opportunity or experience became real for you. The Course says that joy is of the Holy Spirit (T-4.VI.5:6). Think of any time when you were truly inspired and I'm sure you think of it as a time of great joy.

To inspire means to arouse by divine influence, to stimulate to action, to motivate, to effect, or to stimulate energies. When we are inspired natural energy runs through us. There is no reason to be stressed or upset. Just like everyone else, creative, dedicated, inspired individuals have problems, but they do not focus on pathology. They go beyond pathology and look at what can be done.

Because they are inspired and know how to proceed, the question of failure does not arise for inspired individuals. Inspired people do not worry. They get on with their lives, doing what they understand they are here to do.

> *The result of genuine devotion is inspiration,*
> *a word which properly understood is the opposite of fatigue.*
> *To be fatigued is to be dis-spirited,*
> *but to be inspired is to be in the spirit.*
> *To be egocentric is to be dis-spirited,*
> *but to be Self-centered in the right sense*
> *is to be inspired or in spirit.*
> *The truly inspired are enlightened*
> *and cannot abide in darkness.*
>
> —T-4.15:8

Inspiration and Clarity

Inspired individuals can be recognized by a high level of dedication, passion, and devotion. Jesus never did anything half way. Inspired, creative people are also committed people. There is some problem they want to overcome or task they want to fulfill, and they set about doing it. "Inspiration is of the Holy Spirit and certainty is of God according to His laws" (T-7.IV.1:2).

Truly inspired people *know* of the presence of Spirit in their lives. People who are really inspired *know* their goals are certain, often from a very early age. When we are inspired, we feel *called* to do what we do. Though discouraged by parents, teachers, husbands, wives, superiors, or colleagues, inspired individuals go ahead with clarity and do what they do without complaint. Clarity and commitment lead to accomplishment.

As a man and also one of God's creations,
my right thinking,
which came from the Holy Spirit or Universal Inspiration,
taught me first and foremost that this Inspiration is for all.
I could not have it myself without knowing this.
The word "know" is proper in this context,
because the Holy Spirit is so close to knowledge
that He calls it forth; or better, allows it to come.
I have spoken before of the higher or "true" perception,
which is so near to truth that God Himself
can flow across the little gap.
Knowledge is always ready to flow everywhere,
but it cannot oppose.
Therefore you can obstruct it, although you can never lose it.

—T-5.I.4:6

The Holy Spirit—Your Own Inner Self

The fact that God's Voice is quiet, subtle, and always there means that, eventually, it is the Voice we will hear because it is infinitely patient. The Holy Spirit literally has all the time in the world, so He will eventually get through. The ego's voice, which shrieks in terror and takes away our peace, will eventually be stilled, if for no other reason than that we will eventually become exhausted by listening to it and realize that *there must be another way.*

We cannot hear the Voice of our inner guide till we learn to shut out or shut down the shrieking of the ego. It's not the stuff of this world, it's not just television, traffic, and other people that get in the way of our hearing; it's our own inner chatter that we must learn to lay aside, for we ourselves perpetuate distraction. If you wanted to, you could meditate on the corner of 42nd Street and Broadway in New York City, and the noise around you would be like music to your ears. You can be alone in the still darkness of your bedroom and your ego mind can be shrieking with so much terror that you will not be able to sleep.

When you listen to the Holy Spirit, you are also listening to your own Voice — the Mind of Christ with which you are already one. The Holy Spirit is not someone separate from us. The Holy Spirit is us, is you, is me. When we really do what we are called to do, it is our Self that is making the call. When we really do what God wants us to do, we find it is what we also want to do. There is really nothing else that we could possibly want to do. We should "...ask the Holy Spirit everything, and leave all decisions to His gentle counsel" (T-14.III.12:6).

Despite the frequent suggestion of the Course that we should ask the Holy Spirit for His counsel, most Course students will tell you that they do not feel they are very good at asking or listening. I remember once back in the early days of the Course, when I was trying to make a decision and was talking to Dr. Wapnick about my decision-making process, he said: "Well, have you asked?" I responded: "I don't think I'm very good at asking." He just laughed, for the truth is that very few of us are very good at asking.

Very few hear the Voice for God at all because very few of us are accustomed to listening to our inner guide; we are much more accustomed to listening to our own egos:

> *Remember that the Holy Spirit is the Answer,*
> *not the question. The ego always speaks first.*
> *It is capricious and does not mean its maker well.*
> *It believes, and correctly,*
> *that its maker may withdraw his support from it at any moment.*
> *If it meant you well it would be glad,*
> *as the Holy Spirit will be glad when He has brought you home and you*
>   *no longer need His guidance.*
> *The ego does not regard itself as part of you.*
> *Herein lies its primary error,*
> *the foundation of its whole thought system.*

> —T-6.IV.1:1–7

Deciding with God

Even when we think the voice is that of the Holy Spirit, we should double-check, for it may still be our own ego. Whenever the topic of decision-making comes up, the Course always says, "Let the Holy Spirit decide." If we really believe that the Holy Spirit is in charge, then we know He cannot make any mistakes. We can make mistakes but He cannot. If He cannot make a mistake and we turn our decision-making over to Him fully, then we cannot make a mistake either. When we have learned how to decide with God, all decision-making becomes as easy as breathing and we are led as gently as if we were guided down a quiet path. The Holy Spirit will not delay in answering our every question. He knows.

And He will tell us. This is more restful than sleep. We can bring our guilt into sleeping, but not into this (T-14.IV.6:1–4).

Trying to do so leads to increasing anxiety and depression because we know that on our own we will never get it right. For that reason we need help. The judgment of the Holy Spirit is perfect. There is no doubt about the decision being the right decision when it is in accordance with the will of God.

We are completely incapable of making decisions on our own. Insofar as we do, insofar as that decision is ego-based, it is the wrong decision. So what do we do? We begin by being quiet and laying aside the thought that we have any idea about what the decision is and then we wait patiently for the right answer. When the mind is quiet enough the answer will come.

> *Listen in deep silence.*
> *Be very still and open your mind.*
> *Go past all the raucous shrieks and sick imaginings that cover your real*
>   *thoughts*
> *and obscure your eternal link with God.*
> *Sink deep into the place that waits for you beyond the frantic, riotous*
>   *thoughts and sights and sounds of this insane world.*
> *You do not live here.*
> *We are trying to reach your real home.*
> *We are trying to reach the place where you are truly welcome.*
> *We are trying to reach God.*

> — W-pI.49.4:1–8

Chapter 9

Our Help in Every Time of Trouble

~

The Course describes the Holy Spirit as part of our mind and part of the Mind of God. The Holy Spirit is the link that joins the Mind of God and our own minds. "...The Holy Spirit is the bridge for the transfer of perception to knowledge..." (T-5.III.1:2). We have said before that the ego perceives while God knows. According to the Course, perception is not an attribute of God. His is the realm of knowledge. The Holy Spirit mediates between:

> Perception & Knowledge
> Illusion & Truth
> Dream & Reality

The Holy Spirit is the great connector principle. In this sense, His function is that of "translator of the laws of God to those who do not understand them" (T-7.II.4:5). A mediator is one who reconciles differences and brings about a settlement between conflicting parties. The mediation is between our ego mind that would like to rule and the mind of God — our only home. The Holy Spirit mediates between the projections of the ego and the knowledge of the Spirit (W-pII.7:1:6). The ego interprets and through interpretation inevitably misjudges. The Holy Spirit simply knows, and thus leads us to truth.

> *The Holy Spirit is described as the remaining communication link*
> *between God and His separated Sons.*
> *In order to fulfill this special function*
> *the Holy Spirit has assumed a dual function.*
> *He knows because He is part of God;*
> *He perceives because He was sent to save humanity.*
> *He is the great correction principle;*
> *the bringer of true perception,*
> *the inherent power of the vision of Christ.*
> *He is the light in which the forgiven world is perceived;*

81

in which the face of Christ alone is seen.
He never forgets the Creator or His creation.
He never forgets the Son of God
He never forgets you.

—C-6.3:1–8

The Holy Spirit remembers God. He remembers us. He is therefore the link, the bridge, the translator, the mediator between our minds and the mind of God. It is through Him that we are able to remember God. As the answer to the separation we feel in this world, the Holy Spirit knows that the world of the ego is an illusion and does not play into the illusion. His function is to lead us out of our illusions and help us to undo the division we *think* exists between ourselves and God. As the one who leads us out of illusion, He is our guide.

The Holy Spirit as Teacher

The Holy Spirit is the perfect teacher. He uses what our mind already understands, without going counter to our mind, because part of our mind is still for God. Despite the ego's attempt to conceal this part of our mind, it is still much stronger than the ego (T-5.III.10:1–4). The Holy Spirit would teach us that on our own we do not know what anything is for. The lessons at the beginning of the Workbook are designed to help us understand that we have been looking at everything through "ego glasses" and our understanding of reality is distorted. Though the ego plays a dominant role in our lives, there is still a part of our mind that remembers God. Our task, then, is to remember where our real strength abides.

The ego viewpoint is not only wrong, it is impossible, because in order to judge anything rightly, we would have to be aware of an inconceivably wide range of things — past, present, and future. We would have to recognize all the effects of our judgment on everyone and everything. We would have to be certain there is no distortion in our perception, so that our judgments would always be wholly fair to everyone. None of us is able to do this (M-10.3:6). It is not possible to make a right decision without the presence of the Holy Spirit. The good news is that not every decision we make is the wrong decision, so we can be assured that when we choose rightly the Holy Spirit is present with us.

As it is we do not have the maturity that is needed to do God's Will. You might say we have spiritual learning disabilities. The arrogant ego thinks it can figure everything out on its own. What is needed is true humility, which is a clear recognition that of ourselves we know nothing and can do nothing, but that through Him all things are possible. We have learning handicaps in a very literal sense. There are areas in our learning skills that are so impaired that we cannot progress without the constant, clear-cut direction of the Holy Spirit (T-12.V.5:2).

Eventually we all hear the Voice for God because the ego's methodology is doomed to failure. Try as we might to make it on our own, try as many different ways as we want to, try as often as we want, try it on our own over eons of lifetimes, eventually there will be failure. When all else has failed, we turn to God because there is no place else to go.

> *I have often been driven to my knees in prayer*
> *because I had no place else to go.*
>
> — ABRAHAM LINCOLN

> *Failure is never anything*
> *but an invitation to have recourse to God.*
>
> — ANTONIN SERTILLANGES

Dark Lessons

For each of us there are dark and difficult complexes in our individual psyches, stuck places where we have trouble working our way through to the truth. As we grow spiritually we have to be willing to look at what the Course calls dark lessons — places inside ourselves where we have not wanted to look before because we were afraid. Our task, then, is to ask for courage to be able to look at ourselves more closely than before and to do so with heart and guts and resolution to be willing to change not the world but to change our own mind.

> *Whatever aspect of the soul we neglect*
> *becomes a source of suffering.*
>
> — THOMAS MOORE

Sometimes it takes a huge two-by-four across the face in order to get it. I've had prisoners tell me that it was not till they were arrested and therefore were forced to stop the drugging and drinking and acting out that they were able to begin to look at themselves. For some of them that experience did not come till they were sitting in solitary confinement.

Any one of us who has experienced failure in marriage, business, academics, or any other aspect of life knows that at that moment, if at no other, we are likely to turn to God. This does not mean that just because we have failed in some respect we are suddenly going to hear our inner guidance. But at least we have the opportunity.

It is in setting aside the blocks that keep us from hearing or seeing that real relief is found. Pain is neither fun nor a necessary way to learn. There is no need to learn through pain. In fact, real learning is not possible in pain, but it is possible in the relinquishment of our attraction to pain. If we repeatedly choose to put ourselves in similar painful situations, obviously we still have learned nothing. Gentle lessons are acquired joyously and are remembered gladly. Pain, the Course says, is not of God, "for He knows no attack" (T-11.III.1:5). What gives us happiness we want to learn and not forget (T-21.I.3:2).

The purpose of the Course is not to have us seek the truth. It's to help us find out what is not true. To find out what is not true may strike us initially as an unpleasant experience. However, it is not till we are able to look at our illusions that we can then let them go. Once we have let go of our illusions, truth will automatically take their place — because truth is already there.

Defeat is a school in which truth always grows strong.

— HENRY WARD BEECHER

For everything you have missed you have gained something else.

— RALPH WALDO EMERSON

A setback is really a step forward when we are no longer going in the wrong direction. Say you are trying to build a little financial empire for yourself and suddenly it all collapses. That's great! It's great because the answer never was in building a financial empire, and once it becomes clear that the answer is not in this world, you might begin to look within.

Some of your greatest advances you have judged as failures,
and some of your deepest retreats you have evaluated as success.

—T-18.V.1:6

As it is, we have set up learning situations for ourselves through which we cannot learn. We try to learn through overcoming pain, which is not an enjoyable way to learn. Even then, we have not learned our lesson if we keep repeating the same mistakes. The Holy Spirit will direct us to avoid pain. As it is, we no more recognize what is painful than we know what is joyful. We are constantly confusing joy and pain. The Holy Spirit's main function, then, is to teach us how to tell them apart. The confusion of joy and pain is the cause of the idea of sacrifice. When we follow the guidance of the Holy Spirit, we sacrifice nothing and gain everything.

The ego will seek to persuade us that ignoring God's guidance is more fun than paying attention. It seems easier to slip into denial and forgetfulness than to give our attention to the Holy Spirit. The pleasures of this world are very fleeting, while the pleasures of God are everlasting and cannot pass away. Pleasures of the ego are distractions that are never completely fulfilling. For this reason we always feel as though there is something missing in our lives. Distractions are never permanent. It is important to remember that, while the distractions of the ego may seem to interfere with our learning, the ego can have no power to distract us unless we give it the power to do so (T-8.I.2:1–2).

Resign Now as Your Own Teacher

We move into relationships and then try to figure what to do, what the outcome should be. The ego repeatedly messes things up and then tries to figure out how to get out of the mess it created for itself. It's already too late. No clear-cut goal was established in the beginning, so we seem to wander around trying to find our way out. The Course asks us to resign now as our own teacher. The Course is a course in how to know ourselves. As it is we have taught what we are but we have not let what we are teach us (T-16.III.4:2).

There is a Hasidic tale of a man who had been wandering about in a forest for several days, unable to find his way out. Finally he saw a man approaching him in the distance and he said to himself: "Now I shall find the right way out of this forest."

When they neared each other, he asked the man, "Brother, will you please tell me the way out of the forest? I have been wandering about in here for several days, and I am unable to find my way out."

The other man said: "Brother, I do not know the way out either. I, too, am lost and have been wandering about in here for many days. But this much I can tell you. Do not go the way that I have gone, for that is not the way."

The ego is not going to get us out of the world of illusion. The ego, relying on its own resources, will only create one illusion on top of another. As it is, relying only upon our ego we have no idea how to get out of the morass we have created for ourselves. Nor can others tell us the way unless they have found the way. Even then they cannot help us unless we are willing to learn what it is they have to share. Our inner guide knows the way to freedom. He knows the way because He has already been there. With Him we learn that what God wills for us is our will. Without His guidance we think we know things on our own and decide against our own peace. He has not forgotten it. If we do not forget Him, He will make every decision for us (T-14.III.14:1).

Everything we have learned from the past we do not need. When our peace is threatened in any way we say to ourselves:

> *I do not know what anything, including this, means.*
> *And so I do not know how to respond to it.*
> *And I will not use my own past learning as the light*
> *to guide now.*

> —T-14.XI.6:9–11

The ego will not want to resign as teacher, yet it is only by resigning that there is any hope. As the Course expresses it:

> *To say, "Of myself I can do nothing"*
> *is to gain all power.*

> —M-29.4:2

Resigning as our own teachers will not lead to depression but rather will fill us with inspiration. To ask the Holy Spirit to decide for us is to assume power. Because we think we can run our own lives, we deny the Will of God and the guidance of the Holy Spirit. Yet " . . . the Holy Spirit is not delayed in His teaching by your mistakes" (W-pI.95.8:1). We should be glad we have a guide who cannot make mistakes (M-29.2:12).

There is no dark lesson that God has not already shone His light upon. The solution is already there. The solution is a miracle. Your miracle is already there. The choice for God has already been made; we just need to remember it. We think that the miracle has to happen sometime in the future. God, however, does not see time as we do. The miracle is already present. The decision has already been made. "Those who remember always that they know nothing and who have become willing to learn everything, will learn it" (T-14.XI.12:1).

We cannot learn anything if we think we already know. Only when we recognize that we know not can we receive the peace of God. We must step back and let Him lead the way. Though we do not know the way, there is One with us Who does know. God will not abandon us nor fail to answer us if we ask for help. Because the Holy Spirit has a perspective outside the ego's chaos, He knows the solution to any dilemma that seems to confront us.

We need to decide that we do not have to decide. The Holy Spirit asks us to forget and to remember. We forget in order to remember. We forget the illusory world of the ego so we can remember our true identity as children of God. We need to offer the Holy Spirit our willingness to remember. He retains the knowledge of God and our true Self. We should give up everything that would stand in the way of our remembering, for God is in our memory (T-10.II.2:4).

The part of our mind in which truth abides is in constant communication with God, even if we have no conscious awareness of it. The part that listens to the Voice for God is calm, at rest, and wholly certain. Our task is to listen to the part of our mind that speaks for peace.

Practice, Practice, Practice

God's Voice speaks to me all through the day.

—W-pI.49

Let me be still and listen to the truth.

—W-pI.106

All things are echoes of the Voice for God.

—W-pI.151

The lessons from the Workbook ask us to stop and listen. It is possible to go about, all through the day, listening to the Voice for God instead of the shrieking ego. To do so requires practice. As it is, we are very practiced in listening to the voice of the ego, so changing our habits and listening to the Holy Spirit takes a little willingness, a little effort, a little concentration. Be patient with yourself. Practice, as they say, makes perfect. To get good at playing a musical instrument you have to practice, practice, practice. To get good at listening to the Voice of the Holy Spirit is also a matter of practice. The lessons of the Workbook give us a daily reminder, a way to bring into practice the awareness of the reality of God. The Course mentions our need to practice listening some 291 times.

> *Healing thus becomes a lesson in understanding, and the more you*
> *practice it the better teacher and learner you become.*
>
> — T-11.II.2:1; emphasis added

> *Start now to practice our little part in separating out the holy instant.*
>
> — T-15.II.6:9; emphasis added

> *Your practice must therefore rest upon your willingness to let all little-*
> *ness go.*
>
> — T-15.IV.2:1; emphasis added

> *In your practice, try to give over every plan you have accepted for finding*
> *magnitude in littleness.*
>
> — T-15.IV.4:5; emphasis added

We are so used to not listening that we really don't know how to listen, so we should not be surprised if we don't hear an answer the first time we ask, any more than we should be surprised that we don't hit a dart board the first time we throw a dart or the basketball hoop the first time we throw a basketball. "It takes effort and great willingness to learn" (T-5.II.3:10). While an emphasis is placed on effort, it is really an effortless effort. It just looks difficult in the beginning. Once the responsibility for listening is assumed, it becomes effortless. As someone once observed, the hardest part of study is the application of the seat of the pants to the seat of the chair. In a similar way the hardest part is our willingness to listen. Once we begin to listen the process is not difficult.

> *Success must come gently*
> *with a great deal of effort but with no stress or obsession.*
>
> — Don Juan in the Carlos Castaneda material

Living a Guided Life Is an Art and a Science

Living a guided life can be developed just as you would develop any other ability, like ice skating. Unlike a skill that requires muscles or balance or some other physical trait, learning to listen to our inner guide is a mental task and a matter of willingness and can be developed at any time. We can start listening at any age or juncture in life.

Some Course students seem to take listening to an extreme and tell us ad nauseam just how much the Holy Spirit is talking to them—so much that you cannot believe it to all be true. The Holy Spirit does not brag about His abilities. Guidance is also not about predicting the future. It is not about showing off our psychic powers. It is about learning to be so alive in the moment that the response we give to the world will be loving.

It is important to have some time every day when we stop and do nothing but listen. Let all thoughts go and just be present. The Voice for God asks us to remember who we really are — not fearful, complaining children caught in an illusory world of our own making, but loving and joyful children ready and willing to do His will.

> *The Voice for the Holy Spirit does not command,*
> *because it is incapable of arrogance.*
> *It does not demand because, it does not seek control.*
> *It does not overcome, because it does not attack.*
> **It merely reminds.**
> *It is compelling only because of what it reminds you of.*
>
> —T-5.II.7:5; emphasis added

We don't hear the Voice of the Holy Spirit because it is a peaceful voice and the ego is not accustomed to peace. The Voice for God is always quiet, because it speaks for peace. Peace is stronger than war. War is a loud affair and therefore masks or covers over the Voice of God.

- We cannot hear the Voice of the Holy Spirit when we are angry.

- We cannot hear the Voice of the Holy Spirit when we demand that things be a certain way.

- We cannot hear the Voice of the Holy Spirit when we project onto the world.

Whenever we are fearful, we need to remember that the Holy Spirit is always here to help. We discover that there really is nothing to fear when we place our trust in Him. We are never alone. It is impossible to be alone. The more we place our faith in Him, the more we discover His presence. While the Holy Spirit is always with us, He cannot come into our awareness without our invitation. We always have free will. We can choose for God or for the ego. We can be host to God or hostage to the ego. We know who abides with us by recognizing what is already there. We should not be satisfied with imaginary comforters (T-11.II.7:8).

All healing is release from the past. The Holy Spirit is thus the only healer because "...He teaches us that the past does not exist" (T-13.VIII.1:2). Ultimately, the Holy Spirit brings us home again. He is the ultimate healer. To heal is to overcome the separation. To be complete is to come home again.

Chapter 10

Forgiveness and the Holy Spirit

~

The Holy Spirit has a plan to help us heal our relationships. The plan is called forgiveness. We may think that we understand forgiveness. We do not, however, understand forgiveness unless we practice forgiveness.

There was a father and son in Madrid, Spain, whose relationship had become strained. The boy ran away from home. The father began a search for his rebellious son, to no avail. Finally, in a last desperate effort, the father put a large ad in bold print in the newspaper and let it run for several days. The ad read:

Dear Paco. Meet me in front of the newspaper office Saturday at noon. All is forgiven. I love you. Your father.

The next Saturday at noon, in front of the newspaper office there gathered more than a hundred young men named Paco.

The Holy Spirit has a plan of forgiveness. The ego also has a plan of forgiveness. The ego's plan of forgiveness, however, places us in a precarious position. The ego would have us see error first and then attempt to overlook it. Yet we cannot overlook what we have made real. By seeing it we make it real. We cannot make someone wrong and then try to forgive that person. This is impossible. We cannot create an error and then overlook it. We can overlook only what is not there.

We cannot forgive anything if we have not forgiven ourselves. What we attack and condemn in others is what we attack and condemn in ourselves. In order to forgive we must first stop projecting. To project means "to hurl forth." When we project, we make someone else responsible for what we feel. By placing blame we do not have to look at ourselves. We cannot in all honesty look at ourselves and attack another. Thus Jesus says to the accusers of the woman taken in adultery, "Let the one among you who is without sin cast the first stone." No one could cast a stone. Jesus then says to the woman, "Woman where are your accusers?" She says: "There are none Lord." And he says: "Neither do I condemn you. Go and sin no more."

91

We must first have the *experience* of forgiveness. We must know that we have been forgiven, not because we were bad but simply because we were wrong and being wrong is not bad; it's just wrong. We give ourselves guilt. God gives us grace.

There is a joke told in Miracle groups. A young woman, very upset, went to her priest. "Father, you most forgive me! I have committed a sin."

"What is the sin?" questioned the priest.

"I have committed the sin of vanity," replied the woman.

"Oh, how is that?" the priest inquired.

"Well, every morning I get up and I go to the mirror and I say, 'You are so gorgeous. You are so beautiful.'"

And the priest replied, "Oh, my dear, that is not a sin. It's just a mistake."

Forgiveness Is Always Reciprocal

When we pray to God we ask for something we believe we need but our real prayer can only be for forgiveness. In forgiveness we already have what we need. As we forgive others (for not being what we want them to be), so are we forgiven. We must forgive ourselves first because forgiveness, like the process of giving, is always a reciprocal process. As we forgive, so are we forgiven. The responsibility for paying attention, for listening, for forgiving, always falls back upon the thinker. Every time Jesus talks about forgiveness in the Gospels it is always described (as it is in the Lord's Prayer) as a reciprocal process. "Forgive us our debts as we forgive our debtors." Or as the little boy said: "Forgive us our trashbaskets as we forgive those who trashbasket against us."

When we forgive we are not telling God what to do; we are simply recognizing the process by which forgiveness works — a process of cause and effect. As we are forgiven so can we forgive by not creating a problem in the first place, by not engaging in projection. The Holy Spirit is here to help us. We cannot undo the mess we have made by ourselves; we need help. We must, however, take the first step in order to receive help. Thank God (literally) there is help. When we give up, by turning things over to the Holy Spirit we get help. The Holy Spirit then joins with us to make the holy instant far greater than we can understand. It is our realization that we need do so little that enables Him to give so much (T-18.IV.4:10).

We should never attempt to overlook our guilt before we ask the Holy Spirit's help. Our part is only to offer Him a little willingness to let Him remove all fear and hatred and to be forgiven (T-18.V.2:1–3). Forgiveness as taught by the Holy Spirit does not use fear to undo fear, nor try to make real what is not real. "Forgiveness through the Holy Spirit lies simply in looking beyond error from the beginning..." (T-9.IV.5:3).

Not Making the Error Real

In the movie *A League of Their Own*, about women's baseball during the Second World War, there is a scene in which one of the women makes an error during a game and is reprimanded so severely by the coach, played by Tom Hanks, that she begins to cry. The flustered coach begins to holler, "There's no crying in baseball!" By everyone's reactions he realizes that that is not the best way to handle the situation. When the same woman makes the same error in the final game of the World Series, the coach struggles with himself not to yell at her again. His face is full of anguish and frustration, and he starts to talk, but he cannot find the words. For several minutes he struggles with his emotions and then finally, very calmly, tells her that he'd like her to work on that problem before the start of the next season. She responds with a happy and grateful smile. The scene was a good example of forgiveness, of overlooking the error, letting it go, not making it real.

There is a similar story from football. Several years ago Coach Joe Paterno and his Penn State football team were playing for the national championships against Alabama in the Sugar Bowl. They probably would have won, but they had a touchdown called back because there was a twelfth man on the field at the time of the play. After the game, Paterno was asked to identify the extra player and he said, "It's only a game. I have no intention of identifying the boy. He just made a mistake." In a game like football you can see that it really doesn't mean anything. It is only a game. So it is in the game of life: what we would make important is not important.

Jesus on the cross is showing us that we do not have to make the error real. Though his brothers were killing his body, he did not judge them. We may see the error, but we do not have to compound the error. We do not have to make the error real through our judgments — neither the silent judgments we make in our own minds, nor the judgments we pronounce to the world. As it is, we do not understand forgiveness, for we believe that error must be met with punishment instead of love. Yet all we learn through punishment is a deeper sense of guilt, isolation, separation, and lostness.

I heard a story that correctly exemplifies change in perception and for-

ess. A small boy at a summer camp received a box of cookies in the man from his mother. He ate a few and then placed the remainder under his bed. The next day after lunch he went to his tent to get a cookie. The box was gone.

That afternoon a camp counselor, who knew of the theft, saw another boy sitting in the woods eating the stolen cookies. He returned to the group and sought out the boy whose cookies had been stolen and said: "I know who stole your cookies. Will you help me teach him a lesson?"

The puzzled boy replied "Well, yes — but aren't you going to punish him?"

The counselor explained, "No, that would only make him hate you and resent me. I want you to call your mother and ask her to send you another box of cookies."

The boy did as the counselor asked and a few days later received another box of cookies. The counselor said, "Now, the boy who stole your cookies is sitting down by the lake. Go down there and share your cookies with him." The boy protested. "I know," said the counselor. "But try it. See what happens." Half an hour later the counselor saw the two coming up the hill. The boy who had stolen the cookies was earnestly trying to get the other to accept his pocket knife in payment for the stolen cookies, and the other was just as earnestly refusing the gift from his new friend, saying that a few cookies weren't that important.

The Holy Spirit Cannot Attack or Be Attacked

Attack means nothing to the Holy Spirit because He is a giver of love. The Holy Spirit does not teach us to judge others, because He does not want us to teach error and thus learn it ourselves (T-6.V(C).2:1). We cannot begin to let our judgments go if we do not recognize our repetitive use of them. In the first instance all we have to do is to watch our own actions. Rather than jumping to the gun with our defense, rather than immediately being ready to hit back, we are simply asked to look at our reactions, our judgments, the interpretations we place upon the world and begin to see that we do not need them. They are not leading us out of the morass we have got ourselves into. They only lead us into deeper despondency and despair.

Holy Spirit frees us from all heavy burdens, including the criticism and judgment we carry around inside ourselves. Inspired people don't have time to complain or to judge. When someone tells me they want to make a call or write a letter to give someone a piece of their mind, I suggest they not waste their time. It is better to have peace of mind than to give someone a piece of your mind. Can you imagine Jesus being judgmental because others around him were not as filled with Spirit as he?

Miracles are natural, and when they do not occur something has gone wrong. The natural, miraculous thing is not to judge, not to compound error. The Holy Spirit would have us use our special relationships as supports of the truth. With the guidance of the Holy Spirit every relationship is a lesson in love. The Holy Spirit knows no one is special. Yet He also knows that we have made special relationships, which He would purify and not let us destroy (T-15.V.5:1).

It does not make any difference how *unholy* a relationship we have made. The Holy Spirit can help us turn that relationship into a holy one. I have heard both Dr. William Thetford and Dr. Kenneth Wapnick say that one of their favorite passages in the Course is:

> *The holiest spot on earth*
> *is where an ancient hatred has become a present love.*
>
> —T-26.IX.6:1

Seeing Only the Past

We are asked to give over to the Holy Spirit all of our unholy relationships. As long as we hold on to the past (where guilt resides), we will not be able to achieve the change in vision He asks of us.

> *Everyone on earth has formed special relationships,*
> *and although this is not so in Heaven,*
> *the Holy Spirit knows how to bring a touch of Heaven to them here.*
>
> —T-15.V.8:1

God sees us in our perfection, as does the Holy Spirit. To see us in our perfection requires seeing us in the present. To see the past is to see guilt. To see the present is to see love. We can make someone wrong only in the past. If we really knew others in the fullness of their reality of spirit, we could see nothing on which we could place blame. In the holy instant, freed of the past, we see love inside ourselves. The ego preserves time by teaching us that we have sinned in the past and therefore have to be fearful of the future, of a punishment we think we rightly deserve.

There is a wonderful true story about a Catholic priest who lived in the Philippines, a much-loved man who carried a burden of guilt about a long past sin. He had committed this so-called sin many years before during his time in seminary. No one knew of it. There was a woman in his parish who claimed she regularly spoke with the Holy Spirit and He with her. The priest was, of course, skeptical of her claim, so he said: "The next time you have one of these conversations with the Holy Spirit, ask Him what sin your priest committed while he was in seminary."

The woman agreed and went home. When she returned to church a few days later, the priest said, "Did the Holy Spirit visit you, and did you ask Him what sin I committed in seminary?"

"Yes," the woman said. "I asked Him."

"Well," said the priest, "what did he say?"

The woman responded: "He said, 'I don't remember.'"

The Holy Spirit does not remember because the Holy Spirit does not make sin real or seek to compound error. Forgiveness as taught by the Holy Spirit does not use fear to undo fear or try to make real what is unreal.

Traditional Christianity teaches that the devil is a real, external force that must be fought against and destroyed. Traditional Christianity talks about fighting against powers of darkness, holy wars, and battles against evil forces. As long as we think the answer to our problems is aggression, as long as we refuse to look within ourselves, we will find problems in the world. As long as we seek for devils (enemies) to destroy, we can never find peace.

Even if we destroy our so-called enemy, we will find an even more ferocious enemy lurking within. The ego's basic thrust is to destroy, so we find lots of talk about the need to destroy what is perceived as evil — be it Saddam Hussein, the devil, or our next door neighbor. We need to become aware of the devil (ego) inside ourselves, not so we can destroy the devil but so we can let it go by realizing it is not real.

Seeing the Son of God

The more we perceive and give strength to the Holy Spirit in others, the more we are capable of recognizing the presence of the Holy Spirit in ourselves. We cannot become aware of the presence of the Holy Spirit in ourselves without acknowledging the Holy Spirit in everyone. Seeing the Holy Spirit in others is the way to have the Holy Spirit answer our prayer. Then it is that we are in true prayer, for we can never pray for ourselves alone. What we acknowledge in others we acknowledge in ourselves and what we share we strengthen (T-5.III.3:5). We misuse our brothers and sisters when we see them as sources of ego support.

It is our choice whether our brothers and sisters support our egos or the Holy Spirit in us (T-15.II.4:5). What would you have others see? As we acknowledge the ego in another, we reinforce it in ourselves. We cannot castigate another and not feel guilt. Castigation seeks separation. No matter how much righteous indignation we might have, if we reinforce fear within another, we reinforce it in ourselves. If we reinforce the presence of the Holy Spirit in another, we reinforce His presence in ourselves.

> *Can you imagine how beautiful those you forgive will look to you?*
> *In no fantasy have you ever seen anything so lovely.*
> *Nothing you see here, sleeping or waking,*
> *comes near to such loveliness.*
> *And nothing will you value like unto this, nor hold so dear.*
> *Nothing that you remember that made your heart sing with joy*
> *has ever brought you even a little part of the happiness*
> *this sight will bring you.*
> *For you will see the Son of God.*
> *You will behold the beauty the Holy Spirit loves to look upon,*
> *and which He thanks the Father for.*
>
> —T-17.II.1:7

Part IV

Our Last Remaining Freedom

Chapter 11

The Power of Decision

As a man thinketh in his heart so is he.

— Proverbs 23:7

You have heard that it was said,
You shall not commit adultery.
But I say to you
everyone who looks at a woman lustfully
has already committed adultery in his heart.

— Matthew 5:27–28

Cogito ego sum. (I think therefore I am.)

— René Descartes

Perhaps the most obvious thing about us as human beings is that we think. Animals think, but we don't think of animals as having the power of self-reflective thought. That is, they cannot reflect upon the fact that they are thinking. It is not our bodies (which will die) but our minds and our awareness of our thinking that distinguish us as unique beings in the universe.

The mind is "the activating agent of spirit" (see Kenneth Wapnick, *Glossary-Index for A Course in Miracles*, Foundation for A Course in Miracles, 1993, p. 115). It is the mind that supplies spirit with creative energy. The mind is not the brain. In fact, as a physical organ the brain is an aspect of the ego. Our minds function ceaselessly, never sleeping but continuing to be active in dreams even when the body must rest. Indeed, the mind continues on even when the body must be laid down to its permanent rest.

Who Are We in Relationship to Our Minds?

What is the function of the mind? Who is the decision-maker? Are we our minds or something more? We speak of "our mind" as though we are the possessors of the mind. We think of the mind as something that "belongs to us." If the mind is something that belongs to us, who is the "us" that controls the mind? Who is the decision-maker? Though I've not heard any one do so recently, back in the early days of the Course Dr. Wapnick used to refer to the decision-maker as "Charlie the chooser." Philosophers sometimes refer to this part of the mind as the observer. Whoever we are, we must be something more than the mind.

We have seen that the mind can be occupied with ego (fearful) functioning, which is not a part of God's Kingdom, or spiritual functioning, which is a part of God's Kingdom, or the eternal mind. In the hands of the ego the mind makes illusions; in the hands of Holy Spirit, it can build a bridge to the real world and bring us back to the truth. A miracle is the release of the mind from the imprisonment of illusion, thus restoring us to sanity (T-1.I.33:4). Miracles restore the mind to its fullness. The ego mind is a state of *brokenness*. It is fractured, split off, and confused.

The mind is very powerful. It can be used in many ways. Much of popular positive-thinking philosophy is subtly ego-oriented. The mind can do all the wonderful things the positive-thinking philosophers tell us it can do. Indeed, we can move mountains. But will moving a mountain awaken us to the reality of God or will it deepen our connection with the ego?

You may know of Terry Fox, the one-legged boy with cancer who jogged across Canada. You may know of Jack Schwartz, who has the ability to run a needle through his arm without pain. A workshop program has been developed to help people learn to walk on hot coals. Through mind training you can make millions of dollars if you want to. The mind can do whatever you want it to. What do you want it to do? Magic is the uncreative use of mind. It is possible to do many magical things, but magical things are not miraculous. What is miraculous is our ability to join our mind with God. It is then that healing occurs because we are restored to fullness.

Once the ego is enthroned in the mind it can create a Hitler. Once the Voice for God is enthroned in the mind it can create a Jesus. Hitler is the best example we have of the ego out of bounds. Jesus is our best example of the mind in alignment with God.

Mind Training

The problem is that our minds are very undisciplined, very untrained. The Course is a course in mind training, and our ability to hear the message of the Course is dependent upon our willingness to question our wandering minds, our beliefs and illusions. We have each spent a lifetime of letting our minds wander with our own musings, which doesn't bring peaceful results. As it is, we are much too tolerant of mind wandering and passively condone our mind's miscreations (T-2.VI.4:6).

Those who are insane are those who don't seem to have any control over their minds. When we are caught in such delirium we can create any kind of world we want. The world is full of fantasy, commercialism, and empty entertainment. With all the mind wandering that goes on, it's not surprising that we have come up with descriptions of fearful states of mind like paranoia and manic depression. We have all chosen neurosis. Insofar as we are ego-bound we are all crazy on some level. In our specialness each of us has about us something that is *off course*; places where we are *hung up*, places where we are *stuck*; places where we still *cannot let go*.

In reading Sogyal Rimpoche's *Tibetan Book of Living and Dying*, I was struck by the fact that he places so much emphasis on training the mind. The Course is also designed as a book on mind training (T-1.VII.3:14). "Ah," you say, "but I don't want to be brainwashed." The problem is that we are all already brainwashed and 99.9 percent of the time we listen to the brainwashing that comes from our own egos and from the collective twentieth-century system of glossing instead of listening to our inner guide.

Our monkey minds jump from one distraction to another. We lack focus and the ability to concentrate. There is no thought that is not without its effect. Who is the decider? How are our decisions made? I can recall in more than one instance in counseling hearing someone say, "I can't help it," meaning they did not believe that they could help thinking or acting in some particular way. The truth is that, we *can* help it. We can always help it; we can always change our minds.

The Mixed Mind Is No Mind

Jesus says that a house divided against itself cannot stand.

> *No one can serve two masters:*
> *for either he will hate the one and love the other,*

or he will be devoted to the one and despise the other.
You cannot serve God and mammon.

— Matthew 6:24

We cannot devote our mind partly to the ego and partly to God and still hear the Voice for God. Nevertheless, the ego tries to live in a divided world. The consequence is confusion and fear. "A separated or divided mind must be confused" (T-3.IV.3:4–6). I once heard a child psychologist say that the worst thing parents can do to children is to give them mixed messages. Mixed messages come from a divided mind and give support to a divided mind. A child with a divided mind does not know what to think and will become rebellious to all ideas coming from the parent. As it is, our minds are divided in their allegiance between God's Kingdom and our own kingdoms and we are totally committed to neither (T-7.VI.9:1).

The more conflicted we are in our own minds, the more inconsistency we see in the world and the more suspicious we become. One of the primary characteristics of the ego is doubt and a lack of faith. Someone once observed: "There is nothing worse than a good person with a mean mind." Some religions take upon themselves the task of seeking out sin to offer proof of its reality. If we seek sin we can always find it. If we seek God we can always find Him. The question is, To what do we want to devote the mind? What do we want to find?

> *Become in all things a God seeker*
> *and in all things a God finder,*
> *at all times and in all places.*

> — Meister Eckhart

It's more fun to be seeking out God than to be seeking out sin. Sin will expose itself just fine without our help.

Once the ego is enthroned in the mind, the mind fills itself with schemes to *save the face of the ego*. We can all think of times when we have deliberately lied or been irresponsible and unwilling to face our irresponsibility. It's been interesting as a teacher to see how many students try to cheat to save face. To save face the ego chooses not to look at the truth.

The Power to Decide

The key to understanding the mind is understanding its capacity to decide. The mind is an agent of choice, and in the realm of the mind we can choose for God (right-mindedness) or for the ego (wrong-mindedness). We can look at the world with love or fear. We've been so conditioned to look through the eyes of fear that it's all we see. When Jesus returns from his wandering in the wilderness, the first thing he says is "Repent." To repent means to do an about-face, to look at things differently. The exciting news is that the mind can be changed. Jesus tells us that our will is as free as his, and God Himself will not go against it (T-8.IV.5:12).

Just as we are free to believe that our mind can be separated or split off from God, so we are we free to make the decision to remember God. In every second, says Meister Eckhart, there is "a little spark" a tiny flicker of the remembrance of God. The little spark can ignite the love of God within us at any moment. Truth will ignite the spark. Truth might come in meditation and reflection; it might come in reading some words of truth; it might come through a final irritated, aggravated, and exasperated giving up on the ego because there are just too many trials and tribulations. We can always choose once again.

> *The power of decisions is your one remaining freedom.*
> *As prisoner of this world you can decide to see it right.*
> *What you made of it is not its reality,*
> *for its reality is only what you give it.*
> *You cannot really give anything but love to anyone or anything,*
> *nor can you really receive anything but love from them.*
>
> —T-12.VIII.9:1; emphasis added

Our Self is still in peace, even though our minds are in conflict (T-3.VIII.5:8). At any moment any of any day, — the Real Us that we really are, our true Self, that Little Spark, can choose which direction we will go. We can always change our minds about the mind. If any decision we make makes us feel fearful, we have made the wrong choice and we can choose once again. The decision is right when it leaves us wholly at peace.

Whenever tempted to engage in separation or do something you need not do — to be angry, to lie, to overeat or drink, or to do something you know will be hurtful to someone — try this thought: "I don't have to." You don't have to. You can — that is free will. But you don't have to. We can decide for God just as well as for the ego. It is not a difficult or a painful task. We have nothing to lose. We will be all right. We must, however, trust totally. And remember, we cannot serve God and mammon.

If in doubt about a decision ask: "Is this decision going to bring me peace of mind or will it take away my peace of mind?" Repeatedly choose in favor of the peace, and peace will come. It is a matter as simple as a decision. In his temptation in the wilderness Jesus chose Spirit instead of ego. He chose for God instead of fear. Jesus tells us that his "... mission was simply to unite the will of the Sonship with the will of the Father by being aware of the Father's will" (T-8.IV.3:4).

Our task is nothing more complicated than becoming aware of our Father's will. Once the decision for Spirit is made, the mind is no longer split, no longer a prisoner. It is anxiety-free. Once free, we can extend and receive love and beneficence. Fulfilling God's function, we fulfill our own function.

Reality is an immediate inner experience that is not linear or time-oriented but directly connected. Thus, the journey to God is an inner journey, a *journey without distance*. Only that part of the mind that remains forever connected with God unites us with our true Self. Only that mind is free of fear and illusion.

When I was eighteen years old I remember listening to a positive-thinking record by Earl Nightingale entitled *The Greatest Secret in the World*. According to Nightingale the greatest secret in the world was that "we become what we think about." What we project is what we see. If we project sadness and sorrow, we see sadness and sorrow coming back our way. If we project holiness and hope, we set both ourselves and the world free. Jesus tells us that there is nothing we cannot do, if we do it in his name. To do it in his name is to do it free of fear. If you want to you can perform miracles — but you cannot do it with a divided mind.

Jesus tells us that *thoughts are real things*. We are always putting our thoughts into the world. We are either extending love, comfort, and beauty, or projecting difficulty, sickness, and sadness. We are in a real sense at all times either healing the world or cursing it.

As a man thinks in his heart, so is he.

> *There are no idle thoughts.*
> *All thinking produces form at some level.*
>
> — T-2.VI.9:12–13

Chapter 12

A Little Willingness

~

A pivotal point in making A Course in Miracles a real, living experience in our lives comes in understanding the power of our willingness not to make our decisions on our own but to make them with the aid of the Holy Spirit. We have been trying to make it on our own but we can't; no one has ever made it on their own. Jesus tells us that we must change our mind and not our behavior, and this is a matter of willingness (T-2.VI.3:4).

Free will exists only in the world of illusion where it *appears* that we have the power to separate ourselves from God. It is also, however, because of this apparent ability to chose that we can choose for the Holy Spirit instead of the ego. Ultimately this way of choosing isn't going to work. It never has worked. We can be happy only when we learn to choose with the Holy Spirit. It is then we learn of the peace of God. The Holy Spirit can use all that we give to Him for our salvation. But He cannot use what we withhold, for He cannot take it from us without our willingness (T-25.VIII.1:1).

We can always change our minds. We can always see peace instead of whatever conflict we are seeing in the world. However, giving our minds over to the peace of God is the last thing most of us want to do. Our thinking patterns and habits are as ingrained in us as the accent that characterizes the sound of our speech. If you grow up in England or Brooklyn or Boston, you have a distinct accent. In fact we have a distinct accent wherever we grow up. We could change our accent if we practiced talking like someone from another part of the country. So, too, we can change our minds if we are willing to try. It just takes what the Course calls "a little willingness." Despite our hang-ups, changing things is a simple process. It merely requires a change of mind. We must, however, be willing to change. Here is a sampling of how the Course talks about willingness:

The real world can actually be perceived.
*All that is necessary is a **willingness** to perceive nothing else.*

—T-11.VIII.2:6; emphasis added

107

All that you need to give this world away in glad exchange
for what you did not make is **willingness** *to learn the one you made is false.*

—T-13.VII.4:4; emphasis added

Your practice must therefore rest upon your **willingness** *to let all littleness go.*

—T-15.IV.2:2; emphasis added

Salvation, perfect and complete,
asks but a little wish that what is true be true;
a little **willingness** *to overlook what is not there.*

—T-26.VII.10:1; emphasis added

And all this shift requires
is that you be **willing** *that this happy change occur.*
No more than this is asked.

—T-31.VII.5:3; emphasis added

The Course never uses the word "courage." Courage can be an ego activity as much as one that comes from spirit. The Course does, however, use the word "willingness." Willingness is a mental faculty by which we deliberately chose. To talk about willingness is to talk about purposefulness, determination, and deliberate intention. Determination is our right use of will in the decision-making process. The Course ask us to begin a happy day with the *determination* not to make a decision by ourselves (T-30.I.14:1). In order to make the right decision all we have to do is to want God above all else. That's all. So why don't we do it?

Why Do We Resist God's Will?

1. We resist because we think we would rather do it our own way. God wills for His mind to be part of us. Insofar as we block inner guidance we interfere with His will. Our task is to stop interfering.

2. We resist because we think we are unworthy. Because we think we are guilty, we think we are undeserving of God's love. We need to think better of ourselves, to see ourselves the way we really are as children of God and not the way we've been making ourselves up to be in our own fantasy. We begin to think better of ourselves when we actually engage in the process of forgiveness.

3. We resist because we think we would be weird if we followed God's Will. If we look about us at some of the people who claim to be following God's Will, we might think they are weird and we wouldn't want to be like that. Of course following God's Will is not something weird. It is perfectly natural — just as all miracles are perfectly natural.

In the section in the text on "a little willingness," the Course asks us to think thus:

> *I who am host to God am worthy of Him.*
> *He Who established His dwelling place in me created it as He would have it be.*
> *It is not needful that I make it ready for Him,*
> *But only that I do not interfere with His plan to restore to me my own awareness of my readiness, which is eternal.*
> *I need add nothing to His plan.*
> *But to receive it, I must be willing not to substitute my own in place of it.*
>
> —T-18.IV.5:9; emphasis added

We really are better than we think we are. The sinful, sick, sorrowful soul we've made ourselves out to be is not who we are. Were we to realize who we really are — as Jesus realized who he really was — everything would change.

The miracle of the holy instant lies in our willingness to let it be what it is. And in our willingness for this lies also our acceptance of ourselves as we were meant to be (T-18.IV.2:8).

Once we begin to listen to our inner guide things work out smoothly. In fact, we don't have any trouble in our decision-making. What might have distracted us in the past is no longer there as a distraction. Once there is no distraction, we can get on with doing what we are called to do.

It is not our job to tell the Holy Spirit how to lead us. The Holy Spirit knows far better than we do which way we need to go. God, however, does not interfere with our choice. We can always choose an illusion. We can always choose not to pay attention. In fact, we're very good at it. We've been doing it for tens of thousands of years. Choosing on our own in the Garden of Eden is how this whole mess got started. What is required is simply a *realization*. What is required of us, as it was of the Prodigal Son, is that we *come to ourselves*, awaken from our dreamy sleep, and make a simple decision to forgive and follow His guidance rather than our own.

We Don't Need to Try to Make Ourselves Holy

Recognizing who we really are, doing what God would have us do, we soon discover that we don't need to learn anything. We just need the willingness to be taught. We don't need to create miracles in order to be given miracles. The Course asks us not to attempt to make ourselves holy.

One day many years ago I called up a friend and suggested that we get together. She said she could not because of her schedule. She was getting up at 5:00 A.M. every day, writing down her dreams, doing an hour of yoga, and then meditating for half an hour. She was fasting that week and reading the Bible. "My goodness." I said "What are you trying to do? Reach perfection in this lifetime?" To which she responded, "Yes." This particular woman later had a nervous breakdown. She was trying too hard. The ego was directing the endeavor. All that is asked of us is that we be willing to change. We don't need to do anything first. We simply need to stop confusing our role with God's role. God is the teacher. We are the students.

The ego knows how to use will power to pump it up so that we will look better or be smarter or richer or holier than other people. The Course, however, asks us to stop trying to do things on our own. On our own we can never achieve the peace of mind that is our birthright as children of God.

Our job is simply not to interfere. Our whole problem is that we have been interfering. God is not angry about this. We need not feel guilty about interfering. We could be enjoying a much happier and fuller life if we did not interfere. There is a way we think things should look in our lives. There is a way in which we think things should be done. With our own plan we never succeed. Our own plan will never get us what we want.

We don't even need good intentions. In fact the Course says that we should not trust our good intentions. We all have good intentions. Any one of us might walk around saying:

- *Someday* my house will be perfectly clean and neat.

- *Someday* my desk will be completely clear of clutter and everything will be neatly filed away.

- *Someday* all the bills will be paid.

- *Someday* I will weigh exactly what I should.

- *Someday* I will have extra money in the bank.

- *Someday* I will be free of all negative habits and addictions.

- *Someday.*

Good intentions are not enough. What we need is the willingness to follow the guidance of God.

We don't have to force anything or make something happen someday. What we need is not good intentions; what we need is a willingness to forgive, to let go, to give up manipulation, and rest in the arms of God. Sigh a sigh of relief. Relax a little. We don't have to become great, mighty, holy people. The Holy Spirit will give us our greatness and our might. What the Holy Spirit has to offer us is far beyond our ability to understand in our little musings, in our little attempts to make life better, more meaningful, and more real.

The Great Willingness and the Little Willingness

At several points the Course says of itself that it is actually easy if we are just willing to change our thinking. We've probably all had the experience of having success at losing weight or stopping smoking or dropping some other form of negative habit or addiction. At the time we did it, it may have looked like a lot of effort was needed, but as we worked on doing whatever we had to do we found it got easier; we found that it only took a little willingness to really change things. The Course is asking the same thing of us. We are asked to give up all grievances and offer up our forgiveness. When we do, we see a new world. We are simply asked to demonstrate a little willingness to pay attention to the Voice for God. We are not asked to decide what the Voice should say or how God should sound when He speaks to us. We are simply asked us to demonstrate a little willingness to let God be God and to then get out of the way.

The great willingness we need comes not from ourselves but from God. We just need a little willingness. God will supply the big willingness. Our little willingness combined with God's great willingness brings miraculous results. Our little willingness joined with the Holy Spirit is all that the Atonement requires. We shall never succeed in undoing guilt on our own, but it can be undone as we demonstrate our willingness to turn things over to God. This is where the grace of God comes in.

> *It is not time we need for this.*
> *It is but willingness.*

For what would seem to need a thousand years
can easily be done in just one instant by the grace of God.

— W-pI.196.4:3–5; emphasis added

Our willingness comes in response to a question: "How willing are you to forgive your brother?" (T-29.VI.1). God's vision is given "...quickly and gladly to anyone who is willing to see his brother or sister as sinless" (T-22.II.13:2). As we engage in forgiveness, as we relinquish the past and let go of our attempts to make things happen, as we quit trying to make up the world and just let it be, we discover the grace of God. The Second Coming comes as we demonstrate our willingness to let forgiveness rest upon all things.

Remember:

There is no strain in doing God's Will
as soon as you recognize that it is your own.

— T-2.VII.6:4

It just takes a little willingness.

Chapter 13

Accepting Responsibility

∽

*The **sole responsibility** of the miracle worker
is to accept the ATONEMENT for himself.*

—T-2.V.5:1; emphasis added

Ultimately each of us must respond to the call to be who we were meant to be. No one else can do it for us. In an airplane the authority is somewhat divided between the pilot, the copilot, the navigation officer, and the control tower. And the second officer can relieve and take the place of the first officer if necessary. For the flight of our souls there is only authority. We must each assume responsibility for our own lives.

Travel at Your Own Risk

Sometimes when you're traveling across county you'll see a sign that reads, "Travel at your own risk," perhaps along with other signs like "Road under construction." By posting such signs the highway department not only warns the traveler to be cautious but also absolves the county or state of responsibility in case of accident on that part of the road. If travelers come to harm on the road, they cannot bring suit for damages. They are "traveling at their own risk."

In the journey of life we each travel at our own risk. We are the responsible party. Our friends, our neighbor, our parents, the community in which we live, our schools, our teachers, our relatives cannot make our decisions for us. We do the traveling and we incur the risks. Various proverbs and maxims express this truth in familiar language.

> *Everyone has his own life to live.*
>
> *We are each the master of our fate.*
>
> *We are each the captain of our soul.*

113

Like it or not we must respond to being here. Our sole responsibility is to wake up, to listen to the Voice for God in our lives, to discover ourselves, to come home again, to accept the Atonement for ourselves. To accept the Atonement means to undo the mess we've gotten into. And — face it for a moment — we have all gotten ourselves into messes and we are responsible for the messes we find around us. While we may think that we are responsible for what we do but not for what we think, the truth is that we are responsible for what we think, because it is only at this level that we can exercise choice. What we do comes from what we think. Whenever we are afraid, it is a sure sign that we have allowed our mind to miscreate and have not allowed the Holy Spirit to teach us (T-2.VI.2:5–7 and 10).

The Course, Christian Science, the Vedanta Philosophy of Hinduism, the Church of Religious Science, Unity School of Religion, Alcoholics Anonymous, and various thought systems all place emphasis on the power of the mind. Our task is to give up the idea that there is something outside our mind that is more powerful than our mind.

> *What is the single requisite for this shift in perception?*
> *It is simply this;*
> *the recognition that sickness is of the mind,*
> *and has nothing to do with the body.*
> *What does this recognition "cost"?*
> *It costs the whole world you see,*
> *for the world will never again appear to rule the mind.*
> *For with this recognition is responsibility placed where it belongs;*
> *not with the world,*
> *but on him who looks on the world and sees it as it is not.*
>
> —M-5.II.3:1–5

Once you accept the premise that the world is as you make it and nothing more than that, then you know you are responsible for whatever experience comes your way. If I get into financial difficulty, I'm the one who got into that difficulty. If I get into trouble in my relationships, I'm the one that got into trouble and I must work on healing that relationship.

My students in prison might tell me it was society, the courts, their parents, or their girlfriends or wives who were responsible for their misfortune. It is easy to pass the buck; the ego is very good at it. We cannot begin to change things until we accept responsibility for absolutely every-

thing that seems to happens to us. To accept responsibility is the s̲ᷓ
realization that we are accountable for whatever has happened in our life.
As Harry Truman said it: "The buck stops here!"

To respond to the circumstances of our lives gives us strength. As Wen-
dell Phillips says, "Responsibility educates." The more responsible we are,
the more capable we are of responding at yet a deeper level. None of us
knows how strong we can be until we take responsibility for our mental
and physical health, for our relationships, for our economics, for our general well-being in the world. Someone once said: Those who blame others
for their problems haven't begun their education. Those who blame themselves have begun their education. And those who blame no one have
finished their education.

No One Can Change Our Minds for Us

No matter how much we might like to blame someone else for the ills
we find in the world, it isn't going to work. "Anger always involves projection of separation, which must ultimately be accepted as one's own
responsibility..." (T-6.IN.1.2). Anger cannot occur unless we believe we
have been attacked. If we believe we have been attacked, we can then
justify our attacking in return and thereby abandon responsibility. Yet the
Course is clear that anger is never justified — never (T-30.VI.1:1). This
does not mean that we are not going to get angry or that anger should
not occur. It just means that if it does occur something has gone wrong
and we need another way to look at our anger.

Jesus did not attack those who crucified him. Our reaction to much
smaller forms of attack calls for the same response. It is up to us whether
we make the error real and condemn others or recognize that those who
are attacking are asking for help. There is a section in chapter 20 of the
Course entitled "The Responsibility for Sight." Each of us is responsible
for the way in which we see the world. The whole purpose of the Course
is to help us look upon the world with more loving eyes.

It is not our responsibility to change the world. It is our responsibility
to change our minds about the world.

There may be teachers along the way who instruct us in how to live
better lives, but it does no good unless we learn the lessons. The Course is
a helpful tool, but it means nothing if we cannot respond to what it asks
of us. The correction of fear is always our own responsibility (T-2.VI.4:1).
No one can take our fear away from us. Insofar as we are fearful we demonstrate a willingness to be separated. Getting back to God and trusting

in God once again enables us to overcome that sense of separation. We are ourselves ultimately responsible for the change in mind that will lead us back to God.

"Everyone teaches and teaches all the time" (T-6.IN.2:2). We need to be responsible teachers. The lesson we give the world is the lesson we find coming back our way. Whatever we teach that we also learn. The ego depends upon our minds. As we made the ego by believing in separation, so can we dissipate it by withdrawing our belief in separation. If we project separation onto anyone else we preserve the belief. When we are willing to accept sole responsibility for the ego's existence we will lay aside all anger and all attack. Having accepted the errors as ours we will not keep them but give them over to the Holy Spirit to be undone, "so that all their effects will vanish from our mind..." (T-7.VIII.5:1–6).

This brings us home again. From the beginning of time we have been trying to take two contradictory voices and make it one voice. The image of God in the Bible is very contradictory. On the one hand we hear news of a loving God and, on the other, the Bible tells us that God beats up people who do not do as He asks. This image of God is like that of a parent hitting a child and saying, "This hurts me more than it does you." Such mixed messages lead to confusion, not to healing. The church has tried to say that both of these images of God are one and the same, but it doesn't work. God is one. God is love. There is no other.

Our Responsibility to Our Brothers and Sisters

Once we give our mind over to the direction of the Holy Spirit, trust in God, and are free of fear, we discover our own true Self, which is who we are, the creation and expression of God's love. We must never forget our responsibility to others because it is our responsibility to ourselves. As we give others their place in the Kingdom of God, so we discover our place in the Kingdom. The Kingdom of God is never found alone.

> *Responsibility is the thing people dread most of all.*
> *Yet it is the one thing in the world that develops us,*
> *gives us manhood or womanhood fiber.*
>
> — FRANK CRANE

The deeper we respond to the call from within, the deeper we can yet respond. The more we exercise, the easier it gets to exercise. I may

spend thirty minutes of jogging one week and thirty-five the next
the next. In the same way the less we project the less need we find for
projection. The better we get at listening to the Voice for God in our lives
and doing what we are called to do, the deeper we can go in fulfilling our
responsibility. There is a responsibility we owe ourselves. It is one we must
learn to remember all the time. The lessons may seem hard at first, but we
learn to love our lessons once we realize where they are taking us. Every
decision we make stems from what we think we are. If we believe the
little can content us, we limit ourselves and we cannot be satisfied. Our
function is not little, and it is only by finding our function and fulfilling it
that we can escape from littleness (T-15.III.3:1–6).

Our function is *to be the salvation of the world*. We are the light of the
world. All we have to do is to save the world, and we save the world by
saving ourselves. It's that simple! There is no need to go off on a mission-
ary effort. The first task is to wake up right here, right now in this very
moment, not in some future moment. At this moment complete salvation
is offered to us and at this moment we can accept it. Not for a moment
do we need to wait. It is our one responsibility (M-24.6:2).

All Jesus is asking of us is that we wake up. He is not asking us to
beat upon our breast and ask for forgiveness or to spend long hours in
meditation or to become sorrowful and repentant of our sins. He is asking
us to be aware of the presence of the Holy Spirit in our lives in this present
moment.

> *It is extremely difficult to reach Atonement by fighting against sin.*
> *Enormous effort is expended in the attempt to make holy what is hated*
> *   and despised.*
> *Nor is a lifetime of contemplation and long periods of meditation aimed at*
> *   detachment from the body necessary.*
> *All such attempts will ultimately succeed because of their purpose.*
> *Yet the means are tedious and very time consuming,*
> *for all of them look to the future for release from a state of present*
> *   unworthiness and inadequacy.*

T-18.VII.4:7–11

All we have to do is to wake up right now. Meditation works because
it stills the mind and helps us stop all the ego chatter, but you don't have
to meditate to stop the ego. You can stop it any moment you want.

Chapter 14

Why Not Be Happy?

~

A story is told about Edmund Burke (1729–97), the famous English states-man and political historian. If Burke had been given his way our history might have been different. He was a British official who was in favor of the American colonies receiving representation in Parliament in exchange for taxation. He was also opposed to British imperialism in India. But that is not part of the story. Burke had a friend who was a famous preacher. This theologian was so popular that King George III and the queen went to hear his sermons. Burke, however, never went to hear his friend preach.

The theologian finally confronted Burke and pointed out to him that while he had read much of Burke's work, Burke had never heard one of his sermons. Burke said that his going to hear him might cause a rift in their friendship. The theologian allowed for questions after his talk and Burke was concerned that he might have a question the theologian would not want to answer. The theologian said: "How could that possibly be? If you have a question, just ask."

The next Sunday Burke was sitting in the front pew. Throughout his sermon the famous preacher emphasized the traditional Christian idea that those who are virtuous and good and believe in God go to Heaven, and those who do not believe in God and are not virtuous and good go to hell. He made the point over and over again in many ways.

When it was over Edmund Burke raised his hand and said: "What hap-pens to those people who believe in God but are not good and virtuous? Napoleon, for example, believes in God but is not virtuous and good. Then again, what happens to those who do not believe in God but are virtuous and good like Socrates and Pythagoras, or the Buddha?"

The theologian was stymied. He did not have a ready answer, so he asked if he could do some research and give an answer the next Sunday. For a week the preacher did his research but could not find an answer in all the writings of all the saints. He finally turned within himself for an answer but found none. On Saturday evening he was exhausted and in turmoil, and he still did not have an answer. He was so upset he could not sleep. Finally, early Sunday morning he dozed off and had a dream.

118

In the dream there was a ship leaving for Heaven, and he got on the ship. The ship sailed into a port marked "Heaven." The place was in disarray. There were paper and garbage strewn around the dock. There was no one to greet him, no one to take his bags. He tried to find someone who would give him some help. All the people he approached told him to leave them alone.

He walked down the dingy, filthy streets. He heard an awful noise and saw a group of Evangelists waving their arms and screaming and shouting at each other. He asked a bystander why these men were shouting at each other and he was told, "Because, nobody else will listen." He could not stand it anymore, so he turned around and went back to the port and asked if he could go to hell.

The ship sailed down to hell. He got off and the place was exquisite. The grounds were immaculate. There was a children's choir singing to greet the oncoming passengers. Someone came up and asked him if he wanted a drink before he took his tour. Everybody was there, men, women, and children, all seemed to be enjoying themselves. He was thrilled by what he saw and the ship's captain said: "This is nothing. Wait till tonight when they have dancing and music." When he asked, "How come this place is so beautiful?" his guide said: "Well it wasn't always this beautiful, not till the mystics started showing up."

He then woke from his dream. He went to church and told his dream to his congregation. His interpretation of the dream was that those who are not virtuous and good create hell wherever they go and those who are virtuous and good create Heaven wherever they are.

Now, I have some good news and some bad news. First, the bad news: *you are not going to Heaven.* Now the good news: *you are not going to hell either.* In fact you are not going anyplace. You are already there. Heaven and hell are not any place at all. Heaven and hell are states of mind. We create Heaven or hell wherever we go, whatever we do, from one moment to another. It is at this moment that complete salvation is offered to us. It is at this moment that we can accept it.

> *Atonement might be equated*
> *with total escape from the past*
> *and total lack of interest in the future.*
> *Heaven is here. There is nowhere else.*
> *Heaven is now. There is no other time.*

> —M-24.6:1–7

There is another interesting story along these same lines. A great and powerful Japanese warrior went to the head monk of a monastery. He asked the monk to show him the difference between Heaven and hell. The monk sneered at the warrior and said: "One so arrogant and small-minded as you would never be able to learn the difference between Heaven and hell." After more such abuse the warrior lost his temper and yelled, "I will show you death then," and began to draw his sword out of its scabbard. The monk smiled widely and calmly said: "And that is hell." The warrior at once understood and pushed his sword back down into its scabbard. Again the monk smiled and said: "And that is Heaven."

Happiness Is a Decision I Make

Interfaith Fellowship once sponsored a talk and workshop by Dr. Christian Almayrac, a French physician better known as Dr. Happiness. Dr. Happiness has developed a tool he calls "Be Happy." In this process we look at our thoughts moment by moment and ask, "Is this the thought I am happiest thinking?" If the answer is no, we think of a thought we would be happy thinking and choose that thought instead. In this way, Dr. Happiness suggests, we can live our lives enjoying the happiness that is our basic nature.

The most common objection to Dr. Happiness's idea is that the process is too simple. It seems to me, however, that when we say the process is too simple, we are really saying we don't want to change our minds. I think Dr. Happiness is onto something very important: "Heaven is a *decision* I *must* make" (W-pI.138.12:4).

It would be safe to substitute the word "happiness" for the word "Heaven" if we think of Heaven as the thought of perfect happiness. In fact when we have some experience that is absolutely the best, we say of that experience that it is "heavenly." The Course asks us to be happy and give the power of decision to Him who must decide for God for us (T-21.II.3:6).

God wills your perfect happiness now.

—T-9.VIII.1:8

In the story of the temptation in the wilderness Jesus again and again dealt with the temptations that were placed before him by saying, "Get thee behind me, Satan." He repeatedly chose for God, not the ego. He did not choose to project, judge, or get angry. He repeatedly chose peace of mind. We can also repeatedly make that same choice if we want to.

We can understand Satan as the ego, for Satan is historically known as the great divider, the separator. Satan is not, however, some external force outside of our own mind. As ultimately the ego is nothing, Satan is also *no thing*. What Jesus showed us is that the decision for God can be made. You can make it. It is not necessary to continue to make choices that make us unhappy. We could just as easily choose to be happy.

Instead of living in a world of division the Course suggests our choosing a happy dream that will lead us out of illusion. In the happy dream we acknowledge the power of decision-making and recognize that we are in charge of our thoughts. Two men are standing on a street corner, and a friend drives by in a new car. One man feels envious; the other does not. Two men look at the same woman. One feels lust; the other does not. In the same way we can choose to see guilt and fear or we can just as easily choose for God.

We are whole only in our guiltlessness. We are whole only when we choose for Heaven. Whenever the pain of guilt seems to attract us, we should remember that if we yield to it we will be deciding against our own happiness (T-14.III.3:3). We cannot judge without feeling guilty. If we are in our right mind we will not choose against our own happiness. So it is only when we are not in our right mind that we choose fear instead of love, the ego instead of the Holy Spirit.

Love asks only that you be happy.

—T-16.II.8:8

Who Is in Charge of Your Mind?

If we choose to be jealous because our mate is talking to someone else, it is we who make that choice. We could see it differently. If we choose to be hurt, we are the ones making that choice. Jesus did not choose to be hurt by his disciples' rejection of him.

- Nobody says we have to get defensive and angry.

- Nobody ever forces us to overeat, or drink.

- Nobody makes us adopt a pessimistic attitude toward life.

Each day, each hour and minute, even every second, we decide between the crucifixion and the resurrection, between the ego and the Holy Spirit. The ego is the choice for guilt. "The Holy Spirit is the choice for guiltlessness" (T-14.III.4:2). We are in charge of our thoughts and can think and do whatever we want. We can get caught in our ego and dream a very unhappy dream; we can feel hurt, angry, and rejected. We can choose a higher perspective and see above it all. Each moment we choose to look upon the world with love or fear.

Whatever we believe becomes real for us. If we see ourselves as separate from God we affirm the reality of separation. We cannot, therefore, experience God's love. What is needed is correction in perception. There is only one place and only one way in which that correction can occur. It can occur only within the mind. As Dr. Happiness would express it: Is this the thought I am happiest thinking? Anything other than a spontaneous yes is a no.

Our minds are constantly choosing to miscreate. We are constantly making choices out of fear instead of love. What is needed is not a pumping up of our wills to try to behave differently. What is needed is a new way of looking at things so that we do not continue to make wrong choices. If I change my mind and look at things differently, then I may very well change my behavior — but it does not necessarily follow that if I change my behavior I will change my mind.

Change is truly possible only at the level of mind. If change occurs at the level of mind, many other things can also change. I must, however, change my mind first. We are not faced with a thousand choices, but with only one choice. A divided mind would tell us there are many choices. In truth, there is not even a choice to make, for when we choose for God we find that is the only thing we ever wanted. There never really was another alternative. Choosing depends on learning, and the truth is not learned; it is recognized, identified, intuited, revealed, disclosed, uncovered.

Jesus in the Course says we should make no decision on our own (T-14.III.12:5). Our task is not to make up our minds and then ask for help but rather, in each and every situation, to first ask the Holy Spirit to guide us in our decision-making. Make the decision for Heaven; if Heaven does not come into your experience, something has happened that is not part of Heaven, so choose once again. If you do not like the results you are getting, you have asked a question by yourself, so ask again with the help of Holy Spirit. The Holy Spirit will not thrust Himself upon us. His answer is gentle. We receive help when we lack opposition to being helped.

"Heaven is a conscious choice..." (W-pI.39.8:1). It is a sure choice between truth and illusion. It is a choice in which the fear of hell comes to an end. The Course says, "Heaven is a decision I must make" (W-pI.138). Ultimately, that decision is going to be made. In fact it already has been made. Our happiness awaits only our acceptance of it. We will all make this decision, so we might as well make it now. Why wait for Heaven?

> *Heaven is the decision I must make.*
> *I make it now, and will not change my mind,*
> *Because it is the only thing I want.*

> —W-pI.138.12:4–5

Chapter 15

Becoming Consistent Listeners: The Holy Instant

~

The Course places emphasis upon our becoming consistent listeners. As we develop consistency we begin to notice spiritual growth. "The ego is a confusion in identification. Never having had a consistent model, it never developed consistency" (T-7.VIII.4:7–8).

If you wish to lose weight you need to stick to a consistent dietary and exercise program. If you diet for a little while and then go off your diet, all you get is brief success followed by failure that is often more depressing than the temporary elation that came with a little success. In spiritual growth as in any form of growth, if we want to be successful we need *consistency, coherence,* and *congruity.* The more times you stop smoking, the greater the chance that someday you will actually stop and never start again. So it is in dropping any habit.

Something similar is called for in spiritual growth. We need a little willingness to begin, but we also need to stick with our practice in order to experience ongoing, consistent results. It's not the first time that we sit down and meditate that we notice some peace of mind. It's not the first time we exercise that we notice results in our body. However, when we stick to it, with a little bit of patience and persistence we begin to notice real results. The Holy Spirit has not fulfilled His teaching function until we become such consistent learners that we learn only of Him (T-15.I.1:4). As most of us have spent our lives listening to the ego, it's not surprising that in order to switch over and start listening to our inner guide, we're going to need to practice more than just for a little while; we need to become consistent in our practice. The Course says that the Holy Spirit is consistent in His teaching (T-7.VI.13:5), that the Kingdom of Heaven is consistent (T-6.V[C].1:6); that healing is consistent (T-7.V.6:10).

It takes consistency to live in the moment. The more we can become alive in the moment, the more we find that moment becoming so completely full, so vivacious, so exuberant, so effervescent we cannot then be pulled off course. When the moment is full of God there is room for nothing else. Insofar as we are fearful, we are fearful only of the past and/or the future, but neither exists in a mind that is awake and coherently present in the moment.

> Each instant is a clean, untarnished birth,
> in which the Son of God emerges from the past into the present.
> And the present extends forever.
> It is so beautiful and so clean and free of guilt
> that nothing but happiness is there.

—T-15.I.8:4–7

Take this very instant, and think of it as all the time there is. There is nothing of the past that is meaningful — now. There is no reason for feeling guilty now, for there is no guilt in the present. Guilt exists only in our psychological experience of the past. Holding on to the past keeps us in hell. However, there is no past; thus, there is no hell. In this moment you are completely free, if you want to be.

We cannot feel imprisoned, bound, or chained unless we accept such a limitation into our minds. Your body might even be imprisoned, but if your mind is free, you are free. If you know who you are as a child of God, you cannot be imprisoned though heavy brick walls surround your body. You are free, free from guilt, free from the past, free of the future, free to be you — right here, right now.

If we have time we have change, but holiness does not change. "Change is an illusion taught by those who cannot see themselves guiltless" (T-15.I.10:5). God does not change. Heaven does not change. Who we are in our purity does not change. That which is consistent contains no contradiction, no fact in disagreement with the rest. Your changelessness is beyond time, beyond attack, and without variability. When time stands still, there is no time. There is no change. Then you just are.

How Long Is an Instant?

An instant is as long as it takes to reestablish perfect sanity, perfect peace, and perfect love for everyone (T-15.I.14:1). An instant is the amount of time it takes to trade hell for Heaven. It is as long as it takes to remember immortality. It is as long as it takes to transcend time. In this instant, in any moment, it is possible to be free and so awake that we remember only God.

Mystics describe their experiences as transcendent. Time, they say, stands still. Whatever is going on in the moment is sufficient. Perhaps you've had this experience. It came first for me when I was a boy on our farm in Missouri, walking though a meadow. There was a moment in which everything was perfect, a moment in which I did not want to be any place else doing anything other that what I was doing. There was no fear of any future, no regret of any past. There was just that moment. That moment can occur at any time.

That moment is with us whenever we focus on the task at hand. Then it is as we lose ourselves so do we find ourselves. As Jesus says it in the Gospels, "Whosoever shall find his life will lose it and whosoever shall lose himself for my sake shall find it."

The ego is always trying to find something, to make a name for itself, to establish itself in history. The Self does not care about history. When the past and future fade into the moment, we are free.

> *There is no morning or evening in the Lord.*
>
> — MOHAMMED

> *Do not occupy your precious time except with the most precious of things, and the most precious of things is the state of being occupied between the past and the future.*
>
> — AHMAB B. ISA AL-KARRAZ

Have you not experienced it? Have you not felt it? Have there not been times in which you remember God even for a flash of a moment? One of the things that attracts us to pets is that they seem to live in the moment. Is there a past for a dog? Can it remember when it was a puppy? Can a cat remember when it was a kitten? Animals are attractive because they are here now. They do not hold grudges or grievances. Grudges can be only of the past.

When my dog Cindy was a puppy, if she made a mess on the floor or tore up something I would scold her and she would run under the bed to hide. Within a few seconds she would be back out wagging her little stub of a tail, tongue hanging out as if to say: "Hi! It's all right isn't it? I forgive you. You forgive me don't ya?"

The holy instant is an interval of time in which we choose forgiveness instead of guilt. Forgiveness brings us into the moment. Grievances hold us in the past. In the holy instant there is nothing to cling to, nothing to hold on to; there is no past, for the Son of God is free. Forgiveness is letting go. It is giving up the idea that we could ever have a different past.

You were hurt in the past. It does not matter who hurt you or why. It is gone.

You did something in the past about which you were not very proud. It does not matter. It is past. It is gone. It is of no importance now. It matters now only if you make it matter now — otherwise it simply does not matter. In truth it does not matter. It never mattered. In eternity it does not matter. Forgiving is letting it all go.

The holy instant is a moment in which we choose a miracle instead of a grievance. The ego by definition looks for grievances, but all grievances keep us from the love of God. Love holds no grievance. We cannot hold a grievance and know our Self. If we hold a grievance we forget who we are. If we hold a grievance we think of ourselves as bodies only. Only the ego can hold a grievance (W-pI.68.1:1–4). A miracle is a change of mind. It is a shift in perception away from the ego's view of the world as a place of sin, guilt, and fear. A grievance is a place in which we are stuck in our psychic system, some place we have let fester and become sore and hurtful.

In Charles Bracelen Flood's book *Lee: The Last Years*, he tells of a time after the Civil War when Robert E. Lee visited a Kentucky woman who took him to the remains of an old tree in front of her home. There she complained that its limbs and trunk had been destroyed by Union artillery fire. She waited for Lee to condemn the North or at least sympathize. Lee paused and then said: "Cut it down, my dear madam, and forget it."

There is a similar story told about Clara Barton, who organized the Red Cross. One time a friend recalled to her a cruel thing that had happened to her some years previously, but Clara seemed not to remember the incident. "Don't you remember the wrong that was done you?" the friend asked Clara. She answered calmly, "No, I remember forgetting it. That's all I remember."

We are in pain to the extent that we refuse to open ourselves to the present. To experience a miracle is to undo the past in the present. To undo the past is to let it all go. When we remember God, we cannot by definition be bound to the past. God is not bound and neither are we. In the holy instant we unchain all our brothers and sisters. We support not their weakness, nor do we support our own.

Sogyal Rimpoche in his wonderful *Tibetan Book of Living and Dying* describes what he calls "the true nature of the mind." The following is his way of talking about his first experience of entering into a holy instant.

> *Past thoughts had died away,*
> *the future had not yet arisen;*
> *the stream of my thoughts was cut right through.*
> *In that pure shock a gap opened,*
> *and in that gap was laid bare a sheer,*
> *immediate awareness of the present*
> *one that was free of any clinging.*
> *It was simple, naked, and fundamental.*
> *And yet that naked simplicity was also radiant*
> *with the warmth of an immense compassion.* (p. 42)

Think of any time you have been truly compassionate, and you'll find it was a time in which you were free of your own stuff, your soap opera, your petty concerns, your little aches and pains. In such a moment you lay all such concerns aside because you do not need them. Only then are we really open to the present. Only then can we feel with the other rather than judge the other. Let all our littleness go. Littleness clings to hurt and pain. The holy instant is an experience of magnitude. It is an experience of compassion and joining.

The Opening of the Mind

Sogyal Rimpoche describes his experience as an opening of the mind. The Course also describes the holy instant as an opening of the mind. When the mind is opened we see things in a new way. A closed mind cannot see beyond the self-imposed blinders. A closed system of thought is locked into itself. Our closed eyes keep us from seeing. In the holy instant our eyes are open, and there is no one we would condemn. In a holy instant we cannot by definition condemn anyone, including ourselves, and in that there is great freedom.

The holy instant is a moment in which we receive communication from the Holy Spirit instead of the ego. In the holy instant our minds are open both to receive and to give. When our minds are open to receive communication from the Holy Spirit we are most capable of giving to the world we find in front of us. The holy instant is a time in which we receive and give perfect communication (T-15.IV.6:5). The holy instant is this instant and every instant. You decide when it is. The holy instant is beyond the past and the future and "...it stands in shimmering readiness for your acceptance" (T-15.IV.1:8).

Remember: there is no time in the present for the past.

Chapter 16

Setting the Goal

~

Without a clear-cut, positive goal, set at the outset,
the situation just seems to happen,
and makes no sense until it has already happened.

No goal was set with which to bring the means in line.
And now the only judgment left to make
is whether or not the ego likes it;
is it acceptable, or does it call for vengeance?

The absence of a criterion for outcome,
set in advance, makes understanding doubtful
and evaluation impossible.

The value of deciding in advance
what we want to happen is that
you will perceive the situation
as a means to make it happen.

You will therefore make every effort to overlook what
interferes with the accomplishment of your objective,
and concentrate on everything that helps you meet it.

T-17.VI.4:3 and 5–7

I used to make New Year's resolutions. I tried it many times. I even had a little success, but I never had a lot of success. I would try to do things, but I eventually came to understand that success came in not trying. Trying can be a taxing, tough, and toilsome task.

Resolutions usually don't work when we set some sort of rule for ourselves and then try to follow that rule. When we break our own law we feel depressed. One New Year's I resolved to begin every day by getting up at six o'clock, doing a half hour of yoga and meditating for a half hour, and then having a good healthy breakfast before proceeding on with the day. I succeeded in this task for about two weeks, until I stayed up late one night and then could not get up at six o'clock the next morning. Law-ridden resolutions that require us to do certain things at certain times usually do not work. What can work, however, is the setting of a clear goal and then doing those things that will make that goal realizable.

Clear Goals, Clear Results

There is great power in knowing what we really want. As we become clear about what we really want, we can achieve it. For fourteen years I taught a course called Successful Self-Employment at Westchester Community College. All of the books on self-employment I've ever read say you should have some clear goals before you go into business, and you should not start a business without a business plan. If it's true for business, surely it is true when it comes to running the affairs of our lives. There is an old saying: "Clear goals bring clear results; fuzzy goals bring fuzzy results." To realize a goal it is necessary to determine exactly what we want to receive and exactly what we intend to give in return.

In the section of the Course entitled "Setting the Goal," we read: "the practical application of the Holy Spirit's purpose is extremely simple, but it is unequivocal. In fact, in order to be simple it must be unequivocal" (T-17.VI.1:1–2). Unequivocal means definite, positive, clear, sure. If the goal is clear, the results must be sure. If the goal is clear, it can be accomplished. The goal is everything. The Course says the Holy Spirit will give us "very specific information about how to proceed." Very specific information calls upon us to act one way and not another in every situation.

At the beginning of 1994 I set a goal of losing fifteen pounds. I did not write it down on January 1. I awoke one morning at my mother's home during Christmas vacation in Missouri and said to myself that by that time next year I would weigh 180 instead of 195 pounds. This came to me as a clear resolve and a firm commitment. It was also clear that I would need to follow specific steps in order to succeed.

1. I bought a good scale with a large, easy-to-read dial.

2. I weighed myself at the same time every morning and made note of my weight on a calendar I posted above the scale.

This way I was clear about whether or not I was having success in accomplishing this particular goal.

I needed to become more conscious of my compulsive eating behavior, not eat so much, and exercise more. Our ability to change anything is dependent upon our becoming aware of those thinking and behavior patterns that lead us into repeated failure and those that can lead us into repeated success.

The Course says our "goals must be formulated clearly" (T-4.V.5:3). It was clear to me that nothing was going to happen until I made a decision that I really wanted things to change. I had been overweight for more than ten years, and I tried to lose weight several times before with very little success. Now I was beginning to have success because I was clear about a goal. It was also clear that the first thing that had to be changed was my mind. Bringing about this change in my body also brought about a deeper sense of peace as I began to feel and look better. You know your diet is working when other people begin to comment on you're changing shape.

Making the Goal Specific

The Course says "the Holy Spirit's purpose is simple. That which is simple is easily understood." The Course also says the Holy Spirit will work with us "to make our goal more specific." Making our goals specific, we get clearer results. The Course says that the Holy Spirit will provide very specific guidelines for us.

Were we clearer and more honest about our intention, our goals, and our commitment from the beginning, our results would be very different. They would be sure. When we work within the ego's context, the situation just seems to happen and then we try to figure out what it was for, what should have happened. The ego is disorganized and does not know what it wants; it only knows what it does not want (T-17.VI.2:5). The ego by definition is never fully committed. Not being fully committed makes for shabby results.

The only thing the ego is clear about is what it doesn't want. We know what we don't like and are often fairly verbal in telling others exactly what it is that we do not want. Knowing what we do not want, we are still not clear about what we truly do want. If we know what we want and are committed to it, the pathway is smooth and the process easy even if the task is monumental, even, let us say, if our goal is to lose fifty pounds instead of fifteen pounds.

One of the most interesting characteristics of self-actualized people is that they have from an early age a clear sense of commitment to the accomplishment of a specific goals. Great dancers (known or unknown, famous or not) inevitably say they felt called to dance, singers to sing, writers to write, actors to act, teachers to teach, painters to paint, preachers to preach. Jesus at the age of twelve is clear that he must be about "fulfilling his Father's business."

Sorting Out the False from the True

The clearer we are in the beginning, the easier it is to bring the means into play that help us realize our goal. We come to clear goals by allowing the Holy Spirit to help us sort out the false from the true. As we become aware of what we do not need and let it go, we move closer to the truth. What is true is what we need to meet the goal. The false is that which is useless. The situation has meaning because the goal has meaning.

The Italians have an interesting custom. As midnight as New Year's Eve approaches, the streets are clear. There is no traffic; there are no pedestrians; even the policemen take cover. Then, at the stroke of twelve, the windows of the houses fly open. To the sound of laughter, music and fireworks each member of the family pitches out old crockery, ornaments, furniture, and a whole catalogue of personal possessions that remind them of something in the past year they would like to be rid of. While throwing things away may not clear our mind, it's a good idea to clean up our lives by asking for forgiveness where we need to ask and relinquishing the old in order to make way for the new.

Ultimately, there is only one goal and that is to know the truth. Only truth can be said to cure. Only the truth can set us free. Truth walks hand in hand with forgiveness. If our goal is truth the outcome will be peace. Peace cannot exist without truth and sanity. When we are at peace, it is because truth has come to our mind.

What we all really want is the truth. We want to be at peace. We want our relationships to be holy. That's it. The Course says we can have it and that the process for having it is simple. All you have to do is to be fully committed to the truth and nothing but the truth. The truth is where our soul is; our soul is where the truth is. If the situation is used for truth and sanity, its outcome must be peace. We experience peace because the truth has come into our mind.

Try the following simple exercise. Sit down with paper and pen and write across the top of a page:

I would feel better about myself if . . .

If what? What conditions would have to prevail in order to feel better? It might be something very practical like losing weight or saving money. It might be something more general like saying you would feel better if you got along better with your ex-spouse, which might mean being more truthful and more forgiving. Now think, What would I actually have to change in order to bring about these results? What would I have to do to be a better person than I have been? First it is necessary to begin to think about the things required to achieve our goals.

When the decision is made with the Holy Spirit, our result will be sure. Only then will we know real peace. The only goal we can set and truly achieve is the goal in line with that of the Holy Spirit. Our only true goal must be for the truth. Our only goal is God. Our own goal is love. God, love, the truth, they are all the same.

Part V

The Answer to Prayer

Chapter 17

Asking the Right Question

And I tell you, ask and it will be given you;
seek, and you will find; knock and it will be opened to you.
For everyone who asks receives, and he who seeks finds,
and to him who knocks it will be opened.
What father among you, if his son asks for a fish,
will instead of a fish give him a snake;
and if he asks for an egg, will give him a stone?
If you, then, who are evil,
know how to give good gifts to your children,
how much more will the heavenly Father
give the Holy Spirit to those who ask him?

— Luke 11:9–14

"Prayer is a way of asking for something" (T-5.3.V.6:1). When you pray, are you not asking for something, if not for yourself, then for someone else? We pray when we are in need and in our prayer we try to persuade God to see things our way.

> *The object of most prayer*
> *is to wangle an advance on good intentions.*

— Robert Brault

Two shipwrecked sailors were adrift on a raft for days. In desperation, one knelt down and began to pray. "O Lord, I haven't lived a good life. I've drunk too much. I've lied. I've cheated. I've gambled, I've caroused with women. I've done many bad things, but, Lord, if you'll save me, I promise...."

"Don't say another word!" shouted his shipmate. "I think I just spotted land."

Dr. Jacob Bronowski notes in his book *The Ascent of Man* that success in science does not come until science asks the right question. The answer is always there. First it is necessary to ask the right question. The same might be said of trying to find answers in our lives. It is a matter of asking the right question.

I was talking to the twenty-one-year-old woman who cuts my hair. She was talking about her destiny, wondering about the direction she should take in her life. I asked her if she was religious, and she said no. I've noticed that many people wonder out loud about the nature of their destiny. We all have questions about why we are here and where we are going. An extraordinary number of people are interested in these questions whether they are "religious" or not. Religious or not, they talk about their relationship with God and want to know more about God's role in their lives.

What Are You Asking For?

The Bible says all prayer is answered (T-9.II.2:1). All prayer is answered, but we must be clear about whom we pray to and what we pray for. As ego-oriented little children, we often ask for things that take us off track. It should therefore not surprise us that we do not get what we think we want. God is surely not going to give us something that might hurt us.

> *I have lived to thank God*
> *that all my prayers have not been answered.*
>
> — JEAN INGELOW

Our task is not to seek love but to seek and find the barriers we have built against it. "It is not necessary to seek what is true, but it is necessary to seek what is false" (T-16.IV.6:1–2). We are asked to come to the vision of Christ, which sees that everything is okay. We are not to seek love; rather we need to be willing to look at the blocks we have against love. If you want to ask for something, ask for strength to look at the places in yourself where you still need to work on yourself.

How we choose to look at things makes all the difference in the world. It is easy to become absorbed by fear. It is also very unprofitable. Faith and trust bring us into the presence of God. In the presence of God all we want is God. There is nothing else. There never has been anything else. In trust, in humor, in faith we can see ourselves through any test.

Watch yourself. Notice places where you get *stuck*, where you get *hung up*. The Course is about *seeing* the places where we need to grow, where we need to let go, where we need to lay aside concern and trust in God again. As we become aware of the places in which we are caught and let them go, we can more clearly see that in addition to that crazy part of our mind, there is a part of our mind that speaks for God. When we turn down the volume on station WEGO, station WGOD starts coming in more clearly.

Notice the idea around which you are feeling pain and hurt, the place where you know distress. The place where you think you have been injured is exactly the place to let go. If you let go, you do not get hurt. In fact you are going to get to the truth. You are going to get to know something about the Kingdom of Heaven.

Watch, see the place — now let go. Let go again, and again, and again, and again. Let letting go become a spiritual habit. Let the option for love instead of fear become increasingly clear. We become students of the Course when we begin to practice the Course, when we begin to do what the Course asks us to do. When you catch yourself going crazy about something, ask: "How does the Holy Spirit look at this situation?"

Being Clear about What We Need

The first thing we should do in any situation in which we are uncertain is to sincerely ask ourselves: "What do I want to come of this? What is this for?" (T-17.VI.2:1). The ego's modus operandi is the reverse of this procedure. It moves into situations and then tries to determine the outcome. When we move into a relationship, for example, it is a good idea to ask what we want to come of the relationship. The ego's tactic is to move into relationships and then try to figure them out. The ego, like a little child, does not know what it wants, but only what it does not want. The Course teaches that in fact the ego has only one certain goal — *to search for love and not find it* (T-12.IV.1:4).

What we ask for is what we receive. What are you asking for and of whom are you asking? Before we choose to do anything we should ask if our choice is in accord with the Holy Spirit. If we are sure that it is there will be no fear (T-2.VI.4:9–10). If we feel resistant to asking for help, we can be sure that we want our own way to work and we really don't care what our inner guide has to say. God is ready to respond, to give good gifts to those who seek Him. First we must ask — and not just ask, but ask the right question. Knowing what we want from the outset will enable us to achieve what we seek. Jesus is asking us to pass over distractions that interfere with our goal. Fear can pull us aside and ask us to think things we would never think if we were in our right mind. The success we have in fulfilling our destiny depends upon our willingness to practice steps that lead to realization.

Be quiet. The answer you need will be one of peace. It will help you to *unlock* some place where you are blocked. It will be a freeing experience. When we are quiet enough we hear. With correct hearing, the goal can be achieved. The universal goal is to move away from illusions, fantasy, dreams, judgments, pain, and fear.

We have been in the habit of asking the wrong questions, so we need to develop a new habit. We can begin to ask the right kind of questions. We don't have to force ourselves to do anything. We just have to pay attention. Jesus says that there is a way in which we can receive every day exactly what we need, and he says we should start each day with the resolution not to make any decision by ourselves. Our inner guide will take his rightful place in our awareness the instant we turn it over to him (T-14.IX.10:1).

Maybe You've Already Answered Yourself

One sure way to get the wrong answer is to make up our minds about how we want things to turn out and then ask. In this sense we have not really asked. If we already have our minds made up, what good does it do to ask?

You will be able to tell them by their fruits.

— Matthew 7:16

How do we know the difference between the Voice for God and the ego? Look at the results. If you do not like the results, one of three things has happened:

1. You've been asking the wrong question.

2. You've been asking the wrong teacher, or

3. You've been asking the wrong teacher the wrong question.

So ask again.

Notice if you are getting angry. When anger comes up inside, it's certain we have made a wrong decision. What we want is truth and peace, not pain and hell. We could see peace instead of whatever it is we are seeing.

Notice when you make a decision if the decision leaves you wholly free of fear. When I was twenty-two years old I decided I wanted to get married. I got engaged but was not at all sure I had made the right decision. On an ego level I was too embarrassed to admit my mistake, change my mind, and call off the wedding. It actually seemed easier to get married and then get divorced a year later than to call the whole thing off. After my first marriage I wrote a short story about my experience, which I entitled *Here I Come, Guilty or Not.* I had to be willing to look at the fact that I had acted out of fear and had made some wrong choices. Whenever we make a choice while we are afraid, we are very likely to make the wrong choice. Whenever we make any decision we should ask ourselves: Does this decision leave me feeling peaceful? It should bring you joy. It should be a happy decision. If not: Ask once again.

Notice if other people *are also free of fear about your decision.* Do those around you share the peace you think you feel? When we are married and have children or other family responsibilities, our decisions are not ours alone. Be willing to look honestly at the impact your decision has on others.

Passing through Fear — Martin Luther King

Because Jesus was free of fear, he was able to go to the cross without fear. If the decisions we make do not bring us peace, we are still listening to the voice of ego. If we are listening to the Holy Spirit we will experience nothing but peace. Martin Luther King, Jr., tells a story of once being terribly afraid. His life and those of his family had been threatened. One night when he could not sleep, he got up and went and sat at the kitchen table. He was thinking that maybe he should call off a civil rights march. In the middle of the night, in the dark of his kitchen, he began to pray. He asked, "What am I supposed to do?" This is a very good prayer. Like all prayer, it is asking but it is also a way of saying to God, "I want to see this the way you do."

King then sat quietly in the dark, and there in the middle of the night, despite his terror, he said he heard an inner voice tell him *not to be afraid.* The Voice for God will always be reassuring. He got up from the table with a renewed sense of peace and went on in peace despite the threats that were converging upon him.

Notice: When we are not achieving the kind of things we want, something has occurred that is not part of us. If you are not getting what you want, you still have not placed the problem in the hands of God. You have asked the wrong question of the wrong teacher. Once we cancel our own terms, the right question and the right answer can appear. As Kenneth Wapnick expresses it, "The crucial question, should not really be 'How do I know when I am hearing the Holy Spirit?' but 'Why don't I do what He tells me to do so I can hear His Voice better?'" (*Forgiveness and Jesus*, p. 294).

Taking positive action — engaging in forgiveness, letting go — we begin to hear better and better. We all know when we are off course, but it takes integrity to acknowledge our waywardness. We cannot begin to change our minds until we recognize that we need to ask again and again. The more we stop listening to the ego in this regard, the better we can hear our inner guide.

Be Grateful for Ego Failure

In Plato's *Theatetus*, Theatetus says that he knows what knowledge is. Socrates challenges Theatetus to define knowledge, and Theatetus proceeds to put forth a number of definitions, all of which Socrates shows cannot be definitions of knowledge. At the end of the *Theatetus* Socrates concludes that Theatetus has in fact been helpful, for now we at least know what knowledge is not.

When we do not get the right answer, we can at least be grateful that we no longer need to look where the answer is not. Such was my experience in owning a country inn. Choosing to do so was a mistake. It was not what I was supposed to do. Despite the external losses, I'm grateful for the experience. I'm especially grateful that it is in the past. I don't think I shall have to repeat that error. The good news is that the more ego fails us in this respect, the more we can trust the Voice of the Holy Spirit. Now we are in a better position to receive help. Happiness does not depend on being right. The Course asks us: "Do you want to be right or happy?" (T-29.VIII.1:9) The recognition that we made a mistake can be a marvelous aid in changing our perception. Now we can say in perfect honesty: "I want another way to look at this."

The Course is here to help us start thinking along lines that lead to the Kingdom. Our task is to align our minds with the One Mind — to be able to think free of attachments, judgments, petty ego concerns, and projections.

The answer is right when there is no conflict between act and will. When the answer is right, you know. There is no question. Drop opposition to being helped. We do not have to solve our problems on our own. Happy days are those when we resolve not to make decisions by our-selves. We can ask for help from the ego or from Holy Spirit. Whichever we choose is the one from which we will receive an answer. When our minds are aligned with our Advisor, we achieve what we need. Agreement permits things to happen. Nothing real can happen without union. The Course tells us that "decisions cause results because they are not made in isolation" (T-30.I. 16:5). The kind of day you want is the day you give to the world. Have the day you want and give it to the world.

Chapter 18

What Prayer Is and Is Not

~

If you abide in me, and my words abide in you,
you shall ask what you will, and it shall be done unto you.
You have not chosen me, but I have chosen you,
and ordained you, that you should go and bring forth fruit,
and that your fruit should remain;
that whatsoever you shall ask of the Father in my name,
He may give it to you.

— JOHN 15:7, 16

There is a story from India about a boy who was watching a holy man praying on the bank of the Ganges River. When the holy man completed his prayer, the boy asked him: "Will you teach me to pray?"

The holy man studied the boy; then, gripping the boy's head in his hands, he plunged him under the water. The boy struggled frantically. Finally, the holy man released him. "What did you do that for?" asked the boy.

"Well," said the holy man, "that was your first lesson. When you long to pray as much as you longed for breath, then I will be able to teach you."

Most of us are not very interested in prayer unless the need arises. Thus we come to prayer when we are in sorrow rather than when we are in joy. The first course I took in college as a pre-ministerial student was Beginning Preaching. Jesus never taught his disciples to preach — only to pray.

Prayer is perhaps the most universal of all religious experiences. Devout Muslims pray five times each day. Buddhists, Hindus, Christians, and Jews pray daily. Even atheists pray when they are in deep trouble and become fearful. With all the praying that's going on, it's a wonder things don't work out better. There is no one who has not experienced failure at prayer. When that happens, we can't help but wonder if God is listening.

144

God Cannot Answer Prayers with Illusion

*An individual may ask for physical healing
because he is fearful of bodily harm.
At the same time, if he were healed physically,
the threat to his thought system might be considerably more fearful
to him than its physical expression.
In this case he is not really asking for release from fear,
but for the removal of a symptom that he himself selected.
This request is, therefore, not for healing at all.*

—T-9.II.2:4–6

What is needed at the moment of prayer is not a change in our environment. What is needed is a change in our perception. When we can look on any situation with love in our hearts instead of fear, it is a miracle. Once we look at things differently, the externals may also change, but that cannot occur until our minds have changed.

Let us say you are caught in a long line at the bank. You must make a deposit before your checks start to bounce. And at the same time you are late for an appointment, so you are anxious. Now is a good time to pray. In fact, whenever we have to stand on line, it is a very good time to pray. The task, however, is not to pray that the Holy Spirit will speed up the tellers. That's magic. Rather pray that the mind that is anxious, worried, and upset may be relaxed and healed. Once we are calm and centered, once we have everything in perspective, things have a way of working out.

This is what the Course has to say about magic:

> *Miracles bear witness to truth.
> They are convincing because they arise from conviction.
> Without conviction they deteriorate into magic,
> which is mindless and therefore destructive;
> or rather, the uncreative use of mind.*

—T-1.I.14:1

When I owned the country inn, as the situation began to plummet and the mortgage company began to yell "Foreclosure!" I prayed fervently that I would be able to get out of that situation. I lost almost everything, financially speaking, and was forced to start over at the age of forty-six. Fortunately, the experience literally got me back "On Course." Though it took years to crawl out of the hole I had fallen into, I was able to come out with more clarity and understanding about my purpose and mission than ever before. What was true for me, in that instance, is no doubt true for us all. What we think we want is often very far from what our inner guide suggests we do with our lives.

Much of what we call prayer expresses the ego's anxiety, guilt, and fear. We may pray for money or other forms of material rewards, including physical healing, but prayer is not a magic wand we can wave to satisfy our egos. As Diane Berke expresses it: "God is not a big vending machine." Prayer for things, for status, for human love, or external gifts of any kind is always made to set up jailers and to hide from guilt (S-1.III.6:1).

This is not to say that we should not pray when we are in trouble. It is in fact a good time to pray. But think, what shall we pray for? When the inn began to go down, I did not pray for money to save the inn. My ego could have answered that prayer for me. A loan shark came swimming around and made me an offer. Of course the banks were not willing to help out at that point, and he wanted an interest rate higher than the banks'. If I had taken his offer I would either have been in debt to him forever or he would have taken the inn away from me. If I had saved the inn in this fashion I might still be carrying around a white elephant. I prayed that the right thing should happen, that truth would prevail, and did not trust my ego in this situation. After all, my ego had gotten me into this mess. The booklet *The Song of Prayer* tells us that prayer cannot succeed until we realize that it asks for nothing. It is impossible to pray for idols and hope to reach God. We should ask then for what is already given and be willing to receive what is already there (S-2.I.1:2).

Most prayer is asking that a symptom be removed. What is called for is the removal of the cause of suffering. What is called for is a change of mind, not a change in the world. Once things have changed in the mind, we might notice a change in the outer manifestation of things. It is thus that whenever Jesus heals in the Gospels he says: "Your faith has made you whole." It is a change in mind that makes us whole — nothing else.

Let's Not Confuse Prayer with Positive Thinking

The Course speaks about laws of this world and laws of Heaven, which are very different. One of the ways we can correct the magic-miracle con-fusion is to remember that we did not create ourselves. We forget this, however, when we become egocentric, and this puts us in a position where a belief in magic is virtually inevitable. Since creative ability is in the mind, everything we create is necessarily a matter of will (T-2.VIII 1:1 and 3).

According to the laws of this world, we may pray for physical rewards and success and we may very well receive what this world can give us. There are many examples of people using "positive" thinking or "possibility" thinking or "prosperity" thinking to get what they want. There are many popular preachers who espouse this philosophy, and it is easy to see why they are successful. If we believe in prosperity and work hard to achieve it, we may very well achieve it, but it doesn't mean we are on a spiritual path because material things are coming our way. It also does not mean that we are not on a spiritual path if material things come our way.

It is helpful to remember that the ego can answer prayer. The mind is very powerful and can do incredible things. The question is: Into whose service do we choose to place our minds? You can run needles through your body and not hurt yourself. You can walk on hot coals without getting burned. You can endure long periods without sleep. You can lose forty pounds. We can literally move mountains or amass great wealth. The *Guinness Book of World Records* is filled with amazing feats of mind over matter. These events, however, are not miracles. They are examples of the magical, not the miraculous, use of the mind.

There is much the mind can achieve. There is much power that can be gained through training and exercising the mind. There are plenty of audio cassette tapes designed to pump up the mind. But which mind are you pumping up? The mind that is aligned with God or the mind aligned with the ego?

> *Think not He hears the little prayers*
> *of those who call on Him with names of idols*
> *cherished by the world.*
> *They cannot reach Him thus.*
> *He cannot hear requests that He be not Himself,*
> *or that His Son receive another Name than His.*
>
> —W-pI.183.7:3

We can pray to the ego and receive ego rewards. Insofar as it is not consistent with the truth of who we are, we have received nothing. In fact, we have backed away from truth — a little deeper into illusion. The ego is very subtle. It may persuade us, for example, to go into debt to obtain some earthly reward. The idea may be appealing, but then of course the debt must be paid and with interest.

There is an interesting correlation between positive thinking and curses when it comes to getting things in this world. One of the laws of God's Kingdom, as of this world, is the law of cause and effect. In God's Kingdom this law is understood as: As you give so do you receive. In this world the law is understood as: As we do unto others, so is it done unto us.

Prayer can be defined as: "what we think about all day long." What are you thinking about? If we believe we have enemies, for example, and we seek to curse them and bring hell down upon their heads, then it's for sure we have enemies.

> *Hell cannot be asked for another,*
> *and then escaped by him who asks for it.*
> *Only those who are in hell can ask for hell.*

S-1.III.2:5

Be Aware of the Answer You Have Already Received

One of the reasons we think prayer is ineffective is that we are not aware of the answers we have already received. We may especially not be aware of the answer when it comes to us from our brothers or sisters. It is helpful not to doubt another child of God who shares with us the truth as he or she sees it. The Course asks us not to question our brother and not to confound him, for our faith in him is our faith in ourselves (T-9.II.4:2).

Our friends tell us the truth more often than we are willing to hear it. Are you listening? The Holy Spirit can use your brother or sister as a communication medium. Do you hear what your brother or sister has to say? It is not necessary for someone to be enlightened in order for the Holy Spirit to speak through them. Those closest to us often tell us the truth about ourselves, and we need to be able to drop our defenses long enough to hear them. Listen to your brothers and sisters without defenses. Even when they are not telling the truth, we still need to be able to listen without defensiveness and try to understand why they are saying what they are saying. Try to look through what is being said to the truth that is in them. While they may not know who they are, there is a light in their minds that does know (T-9.II.5:8). We are to trust the light in our brothers and sisters that does know.

A priest, a minister, and a rabbi were talking about the most effective position for prayer. As they were talking, a telephone repairman was working on the phone system in the background.

The rabbi said that it was important to daven (rock forward and backward) as you chanted your prayers.

The minister suggested that the key was in the hands. He always held his hands together and pointed them upward.

The priest suggested that they both had it wrong and it was best to pray on your knees.

The phone man couldn't stay out of the conversation and interjected that he found that the most powerful prayer he ever said was when he was dangling upside down from a telephone pole.

We repeatedly confuse form and content. Form matters not at all. What matters is where the heart is, where the head is, where we are as individuals. How we pray does not matter. The words we say are but symbols of symbols. Nothing matters outside of the way we see it.

Several years ago I had a good friend who worked at the IBM think tank in Yorktown Heights, New York. It's a place where a select group of employees go to spend the day trying to expand their creative minds. My friend said there was a man in an office across from him, and he had noticed that the man had nothing on his desk except for a computer. He asked him what he was working on, and he said he was writing a paper on Einstein's theory of relativity and his work on a unified field theory. He told my friend he would give him a copy of his paper once he had finished it. Several months passed and my friend reminded me of the experience. He told me he had received the paper, and he thought I would be interested in the title. It was called "Nothing Matters."

The only thing that matters is what are we thinking about: Where is the heart? And that is the prayer we each say all day long. Whatever is the longing of our hearts, that is our prayer. Pray then not for things; pray for a change of mind. Pray for peace in your own heart, for that is where peace in the world begins. Pray not for money; pray not even for physical healing. Pray for a healing of a mind that is confused and upset and in need of peace.

An elderly gentleman passed his granddaughter's room one night and overheard her repeating the alphabet in an oddly reverent way. He asked her: "What on earth are you up to?" She explained, "I'm saying my prayers, but I don't remember the words so I'm just saying all the letters. I'll let God put it together for me."

It does not matter what we say or how we say it. Sitting, quieting the mind, and looking out the window, or humming a chant or a hymn with reverence is as much a prayer as any words.

> *Does God have a set way of prayer,*
> *a way that He expects us to follow?*
> *I believe some people — a lot of people*
> *pray through the witness of their lives,*
> *through the work they do, the friendships they have,*
> *the love they offer people and receive from people.*
> *Since when are words the only acceptable form of prayer?*
>
> — DOROTHY DAY

Prayer Is an Ongoing Process of Communion

Let me describe a kind of prayer I engaged in as a boy, though I did not think of it as prayer at the time. Like all farm boys I did a lot of hunting, usually on my own. One of the ways to get game was to simply go out into the woods and stand perfectly still and see what would come along. I thus once played possum on a young possum who walked right up to my boot. There was something interesting about freezing in this way. You had to become completely objective. You had to become a witness and see what was going on without any judgment about what you were seeing. It's an interesting form of meditation to simply let yourself become the observer. See what is going on without judgment, interpretation, or concern for how it affects you. When we start thinking about how what we see affects us, things begin to change. It is not the form of the question that matters, nor how it is asked. The form of the answer, if given by God, will suit our need as we see it (S-1.I.2:6).

> *Watch, and pray always.*
>
> — LUKE 21:36

Dr. Robert Weltman is a part of our Sunday evening study group, a long-time student of the Course and an excellent Course teacher. He spends much of his life in prayer. One evening he was telling us that he had noticed that his prayer life is less and less a matter of his saying anything. It is more a matter of quietude. It is more a matter of listening than talking. More and more he finds prayer to be communion. It is

" . . . communion, not prayer, that is the natural state of those who
(T-3.V.1:4).

> *Look as the Holy Spirit looks,*
> *and understand as He understands.*
> *His understanding looks back to God in remembrance of me.*
> *He is in communion with God always, and He is part of you.*
> *He is your guide to salvation, because He holds the remembrance of things*
> *   past and to come,*
> *and brings them to the present.*

> —T-5.III.11.6

Communion has nothing to do with the sharing of Jesus' body. It has everything to do with sharing his Mind, of being one with him.

When I was a freshman in college I ventured one holiday weekend to a Trappist monastery near Dubuque, Iowa, called New Mellery Abbey. It is a lovely old monastery set on several thousand acres. There I met the guestmaster and was given a room for a retreat. The Trappists have taken a vow of silence, and there was no talking in the monastery except for sales in the gift shop and conversation with the guestmaster. What impressed me about the place was going each evening to listen to the monks singing their Gregorian chants. People from the surrounding area would come each evening to sit and listen to the monks. I had never heard anything so beautiful. I understood none of it because it was all in Latin. Still, sitting and listening to them, I felt as though I was experiencing a deep form of prayer. The words mattered not at all. The guestmaster took an interest in me, as I suspect he did in all seekers, and he came and talked to me in my room until late at night. I made several pilgrimages back to New Mellery Abbey, not only during my college years but after completing seminary and my move to New York.

Jesus says we should pray without ceasing. The parable of the Importune Friend (Luke 11:5–8) and the Importune Widow (Luke 18:1–8) call upon us to be persistent in prayer. Prayer is a process, a movement toward the divine, a deepening of spiritual life, and a freeing of ourselves from the fetters of the world. Prayer can become something we do all the time, something that becomes us. It is communion.

> *We need only call to God,*
> *and all temptation disappears.*

Instead of words, we need but feel His Love.
Instead of prayers, we need but call His Name.
Instead of judging, we need but be still
and let all things be healed.

—W-pII.IN.10:2

Prayer is not a preparation for work
or an indispensable condition for effective ministry.
Prayer is Life;
prayer and ministry are the same and can never be divorced.

— HENRI J. M. NOUWEN, *Creative Ministry*

Prayer is an experience of God at the center of our being. Communion comes not by asking anything but simply by letting Him be. Prayer is not supplicating or entreating God. It's not necessarily the words of the minister on Sunday. It's not magic or wishful thinking. It's not wanting in times of scarcity and lack, nor telling God what we need.

Prayer is
  an offering
    a letting go
      a stepping aside
        a giving up of ourselves
          a means of communication
            a time of listening and loving
              a way of remembering our holiness.

Prayer is
  the medium of miracles.
  It is the voice the creation and Creator share.

Through prayer love is received,
  and through miracles love is expressed.

(Paraphrased from *The Song of Prayer*)

Prayer is trusting. It is a way of living something we do every minute of every day.

It is the means of recognizing the Christ, the indwelling God, inside ourselves.

The path to God is joyful because of the One to Whom it leads.

Pray not for magic; pray not for things. Pray for healing of the mind, for release from fear, and for clearer perception. When you pray, forgive, and you will be forgiven.

> *For now it rises as a song of thanks to your Creator,*
> *sung without words, or thoughts, or vain desires,*
> *unneedful now of anything at all.*

—S-1.II.7:8

Chapter 19

Prayer and Forgiveness

~

The little booklet *The Song of Prayer*, which came to Helen Schucman the same way as the Course, suggests we can think of a ladder of prayer. Though a ladder suggests form, it's more like levels of awareness leading to true prayer.

The first level is the level of our asking out of need. Such prayer always involves feelings of weakness and inadequacy. If we knew who we really are we would not need to ask for anything. Insofar as we are unaware of our identity, we pray from need. We take a step up the ladder of prayer when we no longer ask for things of the world that *we think we need*, but instead begin to ask for what is really going to bring us home again.

> *Prayer as a means to effect a private end*
> *is meaningless and theft.*
>
> — Ralph Waldo Emerson

Jesus says we should pray for our enemies, but what does it mean to have an enemy? At one point in the Gospels he says that our enemies are those of our own house. By "of our own house" he does not mean our parents, our children, or our mates. He means that which is of our own soul. If we pray for our enemies and really believe we have enemies, we limit prayer to the laws of this world. Only in this world can we think of ourselves as having enemies. In Heaven this thought would literally be unthinkable. We have no enemies except ourselves.

If we believe we have enemies, then of course we need prayer. But if we have no enemies we move beyond the first rungs of prayer.

An old minister, on the occasion of his retirement, gave me the following advice: "Preach to yourself," he said. "Only under this condition will your preaching have meaning for others." Preaching is best when it is an honest struggle to deal with the issues coming up in our own life and in the lives of those with whom we work. Preaching is for the healing of wounds, not the inflicting of wounds.

Our task is to pray for ourselves for the mind that is twisted ⌐⌐ that a brother or sister is an enemy. Jesus tells us that prayer at any level is always for ourselves (S-1.II.6:1).

Forgiveness-to-Destroy

And whenever you stand praying, forgive,
if you have anything against anyone;
so that your Father also who is in heaven
may forgive you your trespasses.

— MARK 11:25

Forgiveness is prayer's ally;
sister in the plan for your salvation.
Unlike the timeless nature of its sister, prayer,
forgiveness has an end.
For it becomes unneeded when the rising up is done.

—S-2.IN.1:3

To engage in forgiveness we need to understand what forgiveness is. It is safe to say that no gift of Heaven has been more misunderstood than forgiveness. *The Song of Prayer* describes three common forms of forgiveness that are not forgiveness at all, for they are examples of "forgiveness-to-destroy." Forgiveness-to-destroy has made a scourge of what was meant to be a blessing.

Forgiveness-to-destroy will overlook no sin, no crime,
no guilt that it can see and find and "love."
Dear to its heart is error, and mistakes loom large
and grow and swell within its sight.

—S-2.I.2:1

Forgiveness is an illusion. In the process of forgiving we seek to make error real. Sin is in the eye of the beholder, and who but the sinful need to be forgiven? We should not even think that we can see sin in anyone except ourselves (S-2.I.4:8).

It is thus that we need another way of seeing things, a deeper understanding of what forgiveness is. Prayer cannot be released to Heaven while forgiveness-to-destroy remains in us. Forgiveness-to-destroy can take the following forms.

The Better Person. Forgiveness in the form of a better person stooping to forgive a worse person is not forgiveness. An imperious position of gracious lordliness is not forgiveness. We cannot tell someone else that he or she is steeped in sin and not be in sin in ourselves. This is not union. We cannot forgive and yet despise. Someone once said, "No one forgets where the hatchet is buried." True forgiveness means forgetting where the hatchet is buried. It means forgetting that there is a hatchet. It means not having a hatchet. There is no joining in judgment.

The Martyr. On the second level, those who would forgive do not say they are better persons. They now say instead that we are all sinners. But this still represents separation from God, and condemnation is now brought on the other and oneself. In the role of martyr we let another beat us over the head and we sit and smile in silence. Thus do we bear in saintliness the hurt another gives. It is simply a subtle way of proving the other wrong. This is still not forgiveness.

Bargaining and Compromise. A third form of forgiveness-to-destroy is bargaining and compromise where we say: "I will forgive you if you meet my needs, for in your slavery is my release" (S-2.II.6:2). If we enslave anyone, we put ourselves in slavery. The more the bargaining, the greater the guilt. Giving is giving only when we give freely. As Jesus expresses it in the Gospels: "Don't even let your left hand know what your right hand is doing." You see the need. You respond to the need. There is no question about what to do. Giving-to-get, like forgiving-to-destroy, is not giving. We cannot reinforce guilt in another and not reinforce it in ourselves. Insofar as we reinforce guilt we back into separation.

True forgiveness is an experience that leads away from anger, condemnation, and comparison. When we really forgive we see sunshine, hope, and a future that is bright because we are not holding on to the past. True forgiveness comes to us as a kind of prayer.

Forgiveness-for-Salvation

Forgiveness-for-salvation does not ask for proof of innocence nor payment of any kind. Forgiveness-for-salvation does not argue, nor does it evaluate another. True forgiveness finds a new way of looking at things. True forgiveness sees beyond the surface and does not get caught in pettiness. It looks not for error. A brother or sister in pain is crying for love. What that person needs is love, not attack or revenge. Attack and revenge lead to greater darkness and despair. Whenever we become frightened or apprehensive about anything we should say:

> *I will forgive, and this will disappear.*
>
> —W-pI.193.13:3

As we forgive we experience what forgiveness is. Forgiveness has nothing to do with changing the other person. "Salvation is a collaborative venture" (T-4.VI.8:2). We attain entrance to the Kingdom of Heaven holding on the one side the hand of someone we have forgiven and on the other the hand of someone who has forgiven us.

> *My brothers, join with me in this today.*
> *This is salvation's prayer.*
> *Must we not join in what will save the world, along with us?*
>
> —W-pII.264.2:2

No prayer occurs alone, and we cannot pray for ourselves alone. During the Gulf war with Iraq, I heard a televangelist praying to God, asking God to see that ours was a just cause and asking Him to please help us achieve victory over an evil tyrant. The Muslims are very devout in their prayers. No doubt they were also praying that God would help them to victory over an evil tyrant. Prayer as illusion calls for vengeance. Our prayer needs to be for the overcoming of separation, not victory over what we perceive as evil. Since we are not separated, true prayer represents a generosity of spirit that extends to the highest possible good for everyone involved.

Ultimately, we cannot find joy for ourselves alone. Jesus tells us that we can no more pray for ourselves along than we can find joy in ourselves alone. We cannot hear the Voice for God in ourselves alone because we are not alone (T-9.II.6:1).

> *Again I say to you, that if two of you shall agree on earth*
> *as to anything that they shall ask,*
> *it shall be done for them by my Father which is in heaven.*
> *Where two or three are gathered together in my name,*
> *there am I in the midst of them.*
>
> —MATTHEW 18:19–20

Chapter 20

Beside Still Waters

~

The Lord is my Shepherd, I shall not want.
He makes me lie down in green pastures;
he leads me beside still waters.

— Psalm 23:1–2

Several years ago Paul Steinberg, a good friend and active student and teacher of the Course, died suddenly of a heart attack. Paul was only fifty-eight years old. He was a true and genuine seeker, clearly on the path. When he first got *A Course in Miracles*, he did nothing but read the Course till he finished it. That's how thirsty he was for knowledge. Paul then turned and began to share the Course with the world.

When I heard of Paul's death, it stopped me. For some time I could only sit, somewhat numb, looking out the window. When a friend dies you stop. At such a moment you cannot but wonder about the meaning and purpose of life. Death is here to stop us; if we went on forever we would make up incredible egos with incredibly complex worlds. Death stops you.

When the world is too much with us — when we're caught up in the everyday workaday world of socializing, business, family life, school life, church life, television, radio, newspapers, magazines, bills, doctor's visits — it's not unusual to develop a feeling of uneasiness and a lack of assurance that life is going anywhere or has any meaning. When it's all too much for us, each of us needs to be restored in soul. We need to walk, as the Palmist says, "...beside still waters."

> *So God blessed the seventh day and hallowed it,*
> *because on it God rested from all His work*
> *which He had done in creation.*
>
> — Genesis 2:3

We need to feel free and at peace. When we feel peaceful and free, we have everything. We need to be free of illusions, fearful dreams, and the

158

encumbering thoughts of the world. If problems plague us too much in our home and our work, if it becomes impossible to stop the world, we cannot attain that clarity of perception necessary for true peace. Every now and then it is necessary to put aside our daily pursuits, relax for a while and become recentered. Doing so helps us to become rededicated to the task at hand. Every now and then we need to walk "...beside still waters."

In the summer of 1967, after I had completed my master's degree, I took the summer off and went to Paris to study French at the University of Paris. The summer was fun, and I actually managed to learn at least a little French. I also spent a lot of time sitting on a little balcony overlooking a small park and taking long walks at night along the Seine. It was my way of quite literally walking "...beside still waters."

At the end of that summer I took a forty-eight hour train ride from Stockholm, Sweden, to Narvick, Norway, about two hundred miles north of the Arctic Circle. There I was able to sit for two days on the side of a mountain. At the end of that retreat I was filled with incredible energy and a great desire to become active again, to get back to the U.S. and get to work.

In order to gain direction in life, meditation, prayer, and solitude have always been important forms of spiritual exercise. In all the world's religions the most spiritual and peaceful lives have been lived by the nuns and monks — the Trappists, Carmelites, Zen Buddhists, Sufis, and Yogis who allow themselves long periods of silence and meditation. Silence has always been a precursor to inner peace, for each of us needs time to sit "...beside still waters."

Silence and Perspective

In his book *My Shadow Ran Fast* Billy Sands tells the story of finally finding himself only after he wound up in solitary confinement. Prison is certainly not pleasant, but sometimes it takes an extreme experience to stop us. Sometimes we need something to force us to stop and look — past the surface to the greater reality within.

- Prison can do it,
- the death of friend can do it,
- the breakup of a marriage or romance can do it,
- the loss of a business or job can do it,
- a serious accident or illness can do it.

Sometimes we have no choice about walking beside still waters. Suddenly all the business of life stops and there we are all alone standing "... beside still waters."

While trauma can offer us the possibility of a new way of looking at things, it's helpful not to wait for trauma. We need time for silent inner reflection every day. Sundays are for us to have such time every week. It is also good to have a yearly retreat. Get away for a while, quite literally go off and sit beside some body of water, a lake or river, or out to the beach where you can be "... beside still waters."

I like to take January 1 as a day of reflection. There are no plans for New Year's day. After a quiet brunch it's worthwhile to review the year past and think of the things you would like to see happening in the year ahead. It's pleasant to have this time to walk "... beside still waters."

We need silence — daily, weekly, yearly. Daily meditative study guides such as *A Course in Miracles, The Daily Word, The Upper Room, The Daily Blessing* produce positive transformation because they provide a regular program of settling down and aligning our thoughts in accord with higher principles. They are each a way to walk "... beside still waters."

Be Still and Know

Clarity comes through the inner eye and can occur only when we have learned to be still and know. We cannot hear the Voice for God when we are chattering and complaining. Talking is acquired, as are most of the sounds of our world. Prehistoric peoples may well have felt a greater connection to spirit than we do because life was simpler: there was less stimulation, distraction, and need for neurosis; the bills did not have to be paid, the refrigerator did not break down, the kids did not have to be chauffeured. Still today native people have less neurosis and psychosis because they still know how to walk "... beside still waters."

We push our credit cards to the limit. We buy things like cars to give us greater freedom and then are faced with the responsibilities of owning a car. We may have to work harder to earn money to pay for the rising costs of insurance, gas, maintenance, repairs. There is nothing wrong in working hard and earning a good living, but when earning a good living gets in the way of living a good life — when there is no inner life, but only the external — then it is necessary to stop the world to walk "... beside still waters."

Mornings are important times of reflection for to me. Perhaps they are for you.

Morning is when I am awake
and there is a dawn in me.

— HENRY DAVID THOREAU

I love the silence, the time to read through a daily exercise from the Course, or just sit and look out the window. Some people get up in the morning to the news on the radio or they turn on the television.

Millions begin each day by hopping into a car, turning on the radio again, and proceeding to a noisy expressway. Or they dash down the street, stopping to grab a newspaper before jumping into a bus, subway, or taxi. We're all going someplace, and it's important to arrive before our bosses and other employees. Living this way, there is little time to walk "...beside still waters."

Perhaps the deepest reason why we are afraid of death is because we do not know who we are. We believe in a personal, unique, and separate identity; but if we dare to examine it, we find that identity depends entirely on an endless collection of things to prop it up; our name, our "biography," our partners, family, home, job, friends, credit cards.... It is on their fragile and transient support that we rely for our security. So when they are all taken away, will we have any idea of who we really are?

Without our familiar props, we are faced with just ourselves, a person who we do not know, an unnerving stranger with whom we have been living all the time but we never really wanted to meet. Isn't that why we have tried to fill every moment of time with noise and activity, however boring or trivial, to ensure that we are never left in silence with this stranger on our own?

— SOGYAL RIMPOCHE, *The Tibetan Book of Living and Dying,* P. 16

This world offers us a myriad of forms for avoiding looking at ourselves. Yet our true Self unencumbered with ego is the best friend we have, for it is the Self that knows how to listen to the Voice for God. It is to this self that we will eventually pay attention.

The five colors can blind,
the five tones deafen,
the five tastes cloy.
The race, the hunt, can drive men mad
and their booty leaves them no peace.

Therefore the sensible man
prefers the inner to the outer eye.

— Tao Te Ching

Drop Talking

Needing desperately to figure things out, we consult psychiatrists or watch impassioned television preachers telling us about what is the right and wrong thing to do. Or we call friends on the phone. Often we just receive more words, opinions, and increasing confusion.

After my death experience I found I could not talk for a full two hours. I could not talk because I understood that anything I said was a construct, a making up of something, an interpretation. For a while at least there was nothing to interpret. What we need is not more talking, not more words; we need simply to take the Lord's hand and walk "...beside still waters."

Politicians, ministers, lawyers, talk show hosts and participants, businessmen and businesswomen are often busy thinking of something to say. The more caught we are in this world and the soap opera of everyday life, the less chance we have to know the truth that can come only when we learn to be still and know. Have you noticed it? People who talk a lot often have the least to say. Paraphrasing the woman on the television commercial who says, "Help me! I've fallen and I can't get up," one of our former employees used to joke: "Help me! I'm talking and I can't shut up."

Only he who loves silence can safely speak.

— Friedrich Nietzsche

I have often repented of having spoken,
but I have never repented of having kept silent.

— Henri Suso, Christian mystic

Jesus was fond of silence. It's easy to tell that by reading through the Gospels.

And Jesus being filled with the Holy Spirit,
returned from Jordan and was led by the Spirit into the wilderness.

— Matthew 4:1 and Luke 4:1

And the apostles, when they were returned,
told Him all that they had done.
And He took them, and went aside privately into a desert place.

— Matthew 14:13 and Luke 9:10

And it came to pass about eight days after these sayings,
He took Peter and John and James,
and went to into a high mountain apart to pray.

— Matthew 17:1 and Luke 9:28

Then came Jesus with them into a place call Gethsemane,
and said unto the disciples,
Sit here, while I go yonder and pray.

— Mark 14:32 and Matthew 26:36

Getting in touch with personal destiny, doing what we are supposed to be doing, requires periods of doing nothing at all. Jesus frequently found it necessary to leave his disciples and the press of the crowds that fell upon him and go to some quiet place to be alone. He would go off into the desert or the mountains or take a boat out onto a lake. There he would be able to hear the Voice for God. There he would spend his time walking "... beside still waters."

Jesus spoke as one who had authority and not as the scribes and the Pharisees. The scribes and the Pharisees were the "Ph.D.'s" of Jesus' day. They were the ones with prescribed authority. Yet his power and authority surpassed theirs. Why? Because he took the time to walk "... beside still waters."

The kind of peace that characterized Jesus is hard to find in our world of personal and collective illusions. Jesus gained strength with each retreat into solitude, building up to his final retreat in the Garden of Gethsemane. It was this final retreat that gave him the power to face the cross.

Any time we move into silence we gain perspective. You don't have to go off to a monastery. Jesus says that when we pray we should go into our closet and shut the door and pray to our Father in secret, and our Father, who sees in secret, will reward us openly. It can be as simple a thing as a few minutes each morning before we begin the daily chores.

I'm reminded of the clarity of youth, of our life on the farm, of the kind of peace we found on summer evenings, even when we weren't seeking it.

SITTING OUTSIDE ON A SUMMER EVENING

After a hard day of work,
our bellies full of Mother's supper,
the gentle fragrance of
my father smoking a cigar;
talking about nothing consequential;
sometimes not talking at all;
listening to the locusts, katydids, tree frogs, and crickets,
looking — watching darkness fall;
and then the stars, the moon, and the fireflies;
Sleep came so peacefully those summer evenings.

Solvitur Ambulando

I think it is the best of humanity that goes out to walk.
In happy hours, I think all affairs
may be wisely postponed for walking.

— RALPH WALDO EMERSON

The ancient Romans had a saying, *Solvitur Ambulando*, "It is solved by walking." The word "walk" also means "way" or "path." The Bible asks us to walk in the way of the Lord. Walking is an alchemy, a quiet doing. It tones the body, circulates the blood, and brings us energy. It is a restorative, physically, mentally, and spiritually.

There is nothing like walking to get the feel of the country.
A fine landscape is like a piece of music;
it must be taken at the right tempo.
Even a bicycle goes too fast.

— PAUL SCOTT MOWRERE, *The House of Europe*

Perhaps you've had a fight with your husband, wife, or lover. Sometimes when that happens it is helpful for one person to go for a walk. When we are angry we may not know how to find peace, but we can find peace if we are willing to spend some time walking "... beside still waters."

After a little walking you will feel more clarity, more openness, and willingness to share. After a time you can come back again. You can say you're sorry. Your mate or friend will probably be sorry too, and then you can begin again. When friends are upset we may tell them to "walk it off," knowing that when we just walk and let things be, curative powers work within. There may be nothing we can say to help our friend, yet we know they can find strength by walking "...beside still waters."

There is a story about a Zen Buddhist master and one of his students. Each evening they would take a silent walk along the side of a mountain. One day the student asked his master if he could bring a friend the next day, and the master told him that he could but that he should ask his friend not to say anything.

The next evening the student arrived with his friend, and they went on their usual walk. At one point they came to the edge of a bluff looking out on a lovely sunset. Suddenly the friend blurted out, "Oh, what a beautiful sunset!" That is all he said. They completed their walk, and the next day the student returned and the master said: "Never bring that blabbering idiot around here again."

Take a walk by yourself or with someone else on a quiet evening. Let the Holy Spirit's healing power work in and through you. Walk the road, the field, the beach, or a mountain trial. Don't think about anything in particular. See what the deeper part of you has to say. Listen to the Voice for God. Facing the truth, giving up our manipulation, we cannot but find peace. Come back with new authority and then you might truly speak.

We don't have to sit in a meditative posture to meditate. There are many methods. We can go for a run, a bicycle ride, or a quiet time of sailing or fishing. Dr. John Lilly has called driving the American mode of meditation. I remember as a teenager on the farm there were always "Sunday drivers" who would come out from town and drive along looking at the countryside. As a teenager I found it frustrating to come up behind one of them on a narrow gravel road. Still, I knew it was their way of walking "...beside still waters."

> *God never did make a more calm, quiet,*
> *innocent recreation than angling.*
>
> — IZAAK WALTON, *The Compleat Angler*

Walking, fishing, golfing, horseback riding, bicycling, and gardening are all ways any one of us might walk "...beside still waters."

If Jesus found it necessary to move away from the multitudes how, much more necessary is it for those of us who stand at the threshold of the twenty-first century? Jesus' retreats were necessary, and we are not nearly as centered as he.

Each of us needs time in our lives to sit beside still waters. We need to make the time to be very quiet for a moment and allow time for the Voice for God to be revealed to us. There is a kind of inner assurance that can come only when we have allowed for some deeper inner moving.

Go out for a while — take the Lord's hand and walk "... beside still waters."

> *The present state of the world*
> *and the whole of life is diseased.*
> *If I were a doctor and were asked my advice*
> *I should reply Create Silence.*
>
> — SØREN KIERKEGAARD

> *Listen in silence,*
> *and do not raise your voice against Him.*
> *For He teaches the miracles of oneness,*
> *and before his lesson division disappears.*
>
> — T-14.XI.11:4–5

> *His word cannot be heard*
> *Until your mind is quiet*
> *Await His Word in quiet.*
>
> W-pI.125.6:3

Chapter 21

Getting Out of Our Own Way

~

What is the most important step in being able to hear one's inner guide? Do you get there by doing the exercises from A *Course in Miracles?* Does it come in learning how to meditate, in learning to be still and listen? Does it come in studying dreams, hunches, and intuitions? All of these can be helpful, but nothing really begins to change until we learn how to get out of our own way.

Miracles are natural expressions of love, and we need to allow for such natural expressions. But we cannot allow for natural expressions of love if we have things all dammed up. Love cannot flow forth from us when we put things in the way of love. In the same way we cannot hear the Voice for God when we set up interference patterns that keep us from hearing.

Why do we entertain dark lessons? Why are we caught in stuck places? The answer is always fear, and the fear is always of God. We block the love of God from flowing through us because we are afraid to fully admit God's presence in our lives. We are afraid to admit God because we are afraid that if we did there would be nothing of our self left. Indeed, there would be nothing of our self (small "s") left. In all the Eastern religious and esoteric and mystical traditions, we read time and time again that it is not till we are empty of self that we can be full of Self. We're afraid that if God catches up to us we're done for. The truth is that we *are* done for, but it's not till we are done for that we can wake up and begin to live.

The most important element in beginning to apply the principles of the Course is the demonstration of our willingness to do an honest inventory of ourselves and be willing to really *look at, confess, acknowledge, own up to, recognize, admit to* those areas where we have been blocking our own light. Our task is to look at the ego's tricks with the help of the Holy Spirit's nonjudgmental gentleness and patience. We look at these aspects of ourselves not to acknowledge that we are bad but to be free of them. We cannot hear the Voice for God till we have gotten out of our own way. We cannot get out of our own way till we are able to recognize the blocks for what they are and realize that we do not need them. Looking at the ego without guilt and without fear is the essence of the undoing of the ego.

Looking Better

Do you remember the first word you learned in school? The first big word I learned in the first grade reading book — the book about Dick and Jane — was "Look." "Look at Dick. Look at Jane. Look at Sally. Look at Spot. Look at Spot run." The opening chapter of my book *Awaken to Your Own Call* is entitled "Looking Better," it is not about how to be better looking but how to be better in our looking. The Course places a great deal of emphasis on our ability to see things better. As it is, our eyes are clouded over with ego glasses. We don't see things the way the Holy Spirit does because we have prejudices, judgments, beliefs, and convincing interpretations that block our vision. What we have going on is a great deal of ego chatter and confusion.

The purpose of the Course is to help us remove the blocks to an awareness of love's presence. The blocks are all the things we put between ourselves and God, all the negative and hurtful habits, all our prejudices and opinions, all our hiding and projecting, all our sin, all our guilt, and all our fear. So our first step is simply to be willing to admit or recognize that we have all the prejudices, blocks and blinders that keep us from seeing.

We don't want to look in this direction, and most of us have spent a lifetime in denial. When we engage in denial, we try to avoid our guilt by pushing the decision that caused it out of awareness, thus rendering it inaccessible to correction. One of Freud's greatest discoveries was the powerful role of repression and in the ability we all have to bury unpleasant thoughts and memories. As it is " . . . the ego exerts maximal vigilance about what it permits into awareness . . . " (T-4.V.1:3).

What is the first thing that Adam does once he has eaten of the fruit of the tree of the knowledge of good and evil? He hides. He tries to get away from God. When God catches up with him, He asks Adam why he is hiding, and Adam says it is because he is naked — to which God responds, "Who told you that you were naked?" Where did this idea of naked come from? Adam and Eve had been running around naked, but had not the slightest thought about it. Now suddenly there is an awareness of nakedness. Nakedness in this case is clearly associated with shame (guilt), and guilt is manifest in relationship to their bodies.

The fruit of the tree is the fruit of the knowledge of good and evil. A split has entered into the mind. Where there was unity there is now duality and along with that division, discord, disharmony, and fear. Now we need to undo what Adam has done. And of course we are all Adam; we are still engaging in separation. Otherwise we would not be living in a world of duality.

It's not too difficult to see the blocks we put in the way. If we are *willing* to make the stretch to do it. All we need to do is to look at our behavior to see what the blocks are. Any place where our "buttons are pushed," any place we feel guilty, any place we are anxious, any place we are fearful is a place where we are blocked.

Any of the variety of addictions (drugs, food, sex, sleep, etc.) are ways of refusing to listen to the Voice for God. It should be fairly obvious that addicts are running away from something. They are running away from God, and when we run away from God we run away from ourselves. We are still doing what Adam did.

Projection

Each of us needs to ask: By which process do I block awareness of inner guidance? Is it through some form of addiction, through denial and hiding like Adam or through one of our favorite means of not looking at ourselves, namely, projections. Projection is the process by which what we see inwardly determines what we see outwardly. When we project we blame our lack of vision and inability to hear on others whom we claim are yelling so loudly they have drowned out the Voice for God.

The defenses of denial and projection go hand in hand. Both attempt to disguise guilt. Denial hides guilt inside; projection throws guilt outside. When we deny, we simply suppress or repress guilt by pushing it into our subconscious. Projection reinterprets our guilt, telling us that what seems to be our guilt really belongs to someone else, so we blame someone else in order to escape blaming ourselves. When we project we say: "the problem is not in me, it is in you."

Changing the external doesn't change anything unless we change our minds. We may treat an illness with a drug and find relief, but if we have not changed the mind that induced the disease, then the disease will reappear — perhaps in another place, at another time, or in another way, but it will reappear. We have not really gotten out of our own way till we demonstrate a willingness to change the way we look at this world.

> *. . . all your dark lessons must be brought willingly to truth,*
> *and joyously laid down by hands open to receive,*

not closed to take.
Every dark lesson that you bring to Him Who teaches light
He will accept from you, because you do not want it.
And He will gladly exchange each one for the bright lesson
He has learned for you.
Never believe that any lesson you have learned
apart from Him means anything.

T-14.XI.4:5–9

Looking at Our Specialness

Dr. Kenneth Wapnick repeatedly emphasizes the need for us to look at our specialness. It's not just that we think we're special in the eyes of God, but we think we have special problems, that there are special circumstances that make our lives different from others. The truth is that we all have the same problem, namely, the guilt we feel because we think we have separated ourselves from God and thus also from each other.

We need to engage in confession. I'm not suggesting we spill our guts out to the world, dragging up what we may think of as our negative, dirty, ugly feelings, though the honest sharing of our dark lessons with a friend or counselor is not a bad idea. It's interesting which words never appear in the Course. The word "confession" never appears. It's really not a matter of confession; it's not a matter of recognizing ourselves as miserable sinners. It is really the demonstration of a willingness not to keep hiding or projecting our guilt. All we are asked to do is to be willing to quit running away and be willing to look at the ego and see how silly it really is so **we** may then discover that we do not need it.

Ultimately, it's a matter of recognizing ourselves as children of God, but we cannot know who we are till we acknowledge who we are not. We acknowledge who we are not, not to affirm that reality but to become aware of the fact that we are not that. Who we are in truth is something much greater.

We need to demonstrate *a little willingness* to take a hard look at our stuck places. After all, our stuck places are stuck places because we have been unwilling to look at them. We cannot begin to let go of our "stuckness" till we acknowledge that we are stuck. It's not going to be scary; we're not going to lose anything. In fact **we're** going to gain everything.

> *Your willingness to let illusions go*
> *is all the Healer of God's Son requires.*
>
> —T-28.V.10:8

If we don't look we'll be forced to look. Eventually, we'll trip ourselves up, and then we'll have to do that honest inventory. The ego's system has a built-in destruct mechanism. We may try to keep this destruct mechanism from taking effect, but the longer we put off looking at the ego and the more stuff we pile up behind the dam, the closer we get to that day when it's all going to break and come flooding over. It may come out as illness. It may come out in the collapse of a relationship. It may come out as a financial collapse. But it will come out. Communism failed because it has a built-in failure mechanism. What is false will eventually prove itself false, and we don't have to go out on witch hunts to find what is evil in this world. It will come out on its own.

Forgiving the Good

To know God is to know others and to wish them well, for in so doing we wish ourselves well. Our forgiveness must be complete. It must extend to everyone, to what we think of as the good, the bad, and the ugly. Sometimes it may actually be easier to forgive what we call bad than it is for us to forgive what we think of as good — insofar as we think of the good as being better than we are.

What happens, for example, when a friend is successful in a field you have struggling to be successful in yourself? What happens when you are trying to make it, say, as a standup comic and the performer before you does a bit that is so tremendously funny that she has them rolling in the aisles? What happens when you are trying to make it as a singer and you hear someone who has a range and repertoire that exceeds even your highest expectations of yourself? Can we forgive our brother or sister for being better, stronger, funnier, smarter, or more humble than we are? Can we realize these too are judgments we have placed on the situation and all we need to do is just let it be?

> *Nothing gives us quite so much pleasure*
> *as the failure of a friend.*
>
> — MARK TWAIN

Come on, confess it, acknowledge it, we've probably all experienced what Mark Twain is talking about. Were we truly loving that would, of course, not be the case. When we're caught in our egos, it's not unusual for us to be envious or jealous. Maybe we worked harder than someone else for the same result, but because of his connections or because he had resources we did not, he got out of the gate and down the track ahead of us. The process of forgiving what we call good is exactly the same as that for forgiving what we call bad. We need honestly to admit that we have valued something else as more important than God's love.

It does not matter how advanced any of us may think we are. As long as we entertain any fear, as long as we still experience anger or jealously or demonstrate prejudice, as long as we are still apathetic and selfish, we still have work to do on ourselves. Someone once said there is a simple test by which you can tell if your mission in this world is over: if you are still alive, it isn't.

Maybe you don't have any addictions, maybe you don't even have any of what we might call bad habits; still the fact remains that if we are not hearing the Voice for God there must be some blocks someplace. So what is needed is to ask honestly, Where am I blocking an awareness of God's presence? Where do I continue to hang on to my security blanket? overeating? gossiping? lying? Where do I remain stuck? How do I need to change my mind in order to let go of these knots in my psychic system.

There can be no separation. There is no difference between us. Inside we are all colorless, sexless, and free of the differences we find in this world of form. The Hindu word *Sanyasan,* meaning "disciple," is best translated as "colorless." The soul has no color. We are all clear, and clear is not a color. The Course repeatedly emphasizes the fact that we are our brother. Our brother is us. It's in overcoming the separation that we know each other once again.

The answer is always forgiveness. Forgiveness is our ability to look at our specialness with the aid of the Holy Spirit and to do so without guilt or judgment. When we forgive we recognize that no one else is responsible for how we feel or how we act. When we forgive we remove our projections of guilt from our brother or sister. When we forgive, we see that all people are united as children of God.

Postscript

~

Some Suggestions for Listening

1. The primary process for listening is the process of the Atonement, the undoing of our own ego. Notice if you start to go crazy, if you feel hurt or attached, if you think you need to lie. Watch the ego do its thing. See if you can't let some of that nonsense go. As the ego is undone, as we drop our projections and begin to engage in the process of forgiveness, as we get out of our own way, we automatically begin to hear better.

2. Have some quiet time every day when you just sit, with eyes closed or open. Simply spend some time every day being quiet. I like early morning; do it when you can.

3. Use time standing in line at the bank, the grocery, post office etc. to practice meditation. Forget the frustration. Remember, "Infinite patience produces immediate effects" (T-5.VI.12:1).

4. Do the exercises from *A Course in Miracles*. Start on No. 1 and stay with it. It's going someplace. It doesn't matter if it takes two year to do it; just stay with it. There is a difference between reading the Course and doing the Course.

5. Or do the *Daily Word*, *The Upper Room*, *The Daily Blessing*, or any of the daily meditation processes. While I think the Course is the clearest pathway, it's not for everyone.

6. Pay attention to dreams; write them down. Study mythology. Become aware of a deeper inner collective process going on inside.

7. Pay attention to hunches, intuitions, moods, and feelings.

8. Remember something that is worth remembering. Remember something unique. Remember You as the Son of God. Let's let ourselves and others be the very best we can be. I am happy to support your uniqueness and your overcoming of problems. I ask you to support mine.

So you did not grow up in the best of households. So a romance did not work out the way you hoped. So you never got the degree you wanted. We can get hung up any place along the way, or we can forget hang-ups and focus on what is right about life.

Be in love with your mate and children, help them to grow.

Be in love with your work and your play.

Be in love with me. I will be in love with you.

> *And now the way is open,*
> *and the journey has an end in sight at last.*
> *Be still an instant and go home with Him,*
> *and be at peace a while.*

—W-pI.182.12:8

What Else?

If you have enjoyed this book you might enjoy a subscription to *On Course*, a twice-monthly inspirational magazine for the inner journey. *On Course* is published twenty-four times a year and costs $2.50 an issue for delivery by second-class mail or $3.00 an issue for delivery by first-class mail inside a protective envelope. A subscription to *On Course* can be ordered through:

Interfaith Fellowship
459 Carol Drive
Monroe, NY 10950-9565
Tel.: 800-275-4809

Additional Reading

~

Berke, Diane. *Love Always Answers*. New York: Crossroad, 1994.

———. *The Gentle Smile*. New York: Crossroad, 1995.

Coit, Lee. *Listening*. Available from Las Brisas Retreat Center, P.O. Box 500, Wildomar, CA 92595-0500. Lee is also the author of *Listening Still*.

Ferrini, Paul. *The Twelve Steps of Forgiveness*. Heartways Press, P.O. Box 418, Santa Fe, NM 87504-0418. Paul is also the author of *The Wisdom of the Self* and other books.

Hotchkiss, Burt. *Your Owners Manual*. Fernwood Management, 25441 Rice Rd., Sweet Home, OR 97386-9620.

Jampolsky, Jerry, M.D. *Love Is Letting Go of Fear*. New York: Bantam, 1984. Attitudinal Healing, 19 Main St., Belvedere-Tiburon, CA 94920-2507.

———. *Teach Only Love: The Seven Principles of Attitudinal Healing*. New York: Bantam, 1984.

Mundy, Jon. *Awaken to Your Own Call: Exploring A Course in Miracles*. New York: Crossroad, 1994.

Perry, Robert. *Introduction to "A Course in Miracles."* Available from Robert Perry, P.O. Box 4238, West Sedona, AZ 86340-4238. Robert is also the author of *The Elder Brother: Jesus in A Course in Miracles* and an ongoing series of booklets on the Course.

Raub, John Jacob. *Who Told You You Were Naked? Freedom from Judgment, Guilt, and Fear of Punishment*. New York: Crossroad, 1992.

Singh, Tara Singh. *A Course in Miracles: A Gift for All Mankind*. Los Angeles: Life Action Press, 1992. Tara Singh is also the author of many other books. Foundation for Life Action, 902 S. Burnside Ave., Los Angeles, CA 90036.

Wapnick, Dr. Kenneth. *A Talk Given on A Course in Miracles*. A good introduction to the Course. 119pp. Available from Foundation for A Course in Miracles, R.R. 2, Box 71, Roscoe, NY 12776-9506.

———. *Absence from Felicity: The Story of Helen Schucman and Her Scribing of "A Course in Miracles."* 521 pp. Roscoe, N.Y.: Foundation for A Course in Miracles, 1991.

———. *Forgiveness and Jesus: The Meeting Place of "A Course in Miracles."* 348 pp. Roscoe, N.Y.: Foundation for A Course in Miracles, 1985. Addresses the misunderstanding of traditional Christianity and separates these from the teachings of the Course.

Watson, Allen. *A Healed Mind Does Not Plan*. The Circle of Atonement. P.O. Box 4238, West Sedona, AZ 86340.

Williamson, Marianne. *Return to Love: Reflection on A Course in Miracles*. New York: HarperCollins, 1992. Thirty-seven weeks on the bestseller list. Miracles Projects, 1550 N. Hayworth Ave., Los Angeles, CA 90046-3337.

Also by Jon Mundy...

Awaken to Your Own Call
0-8245-1387-8 $11.95

"I have always felt that Jon Mundy does a wonderful job of explaining *A Course in Miracles.*" — BEVERLY HUTCHINSON, Miracles Distribution Center

By Diane Berke...

Love Always Answers
0-8245-1432-7 $11.95

The Gentle Smile: Practicing Oneness in Daily Life
0-8245-1499-8 $13.95

"I celebrate Diane Berke's commitment to teaching higher truths. She is a light that illuminates my life." — DR. WAYNE DYER, author of *Everyday Wisdom*

Of related interest...

John Jacob Raub

Who Told You That You Were Naked?
0-8245-1203-0 $10.95

"A captivatingly simple conversation about a God who always loves and never punishes." — WILLIAM SHANNON, author of *Seeking the Face of God*

Ann Tremaine Linthorst

Mothering as a Spiritual Journey
0-8245-1250-0 $11.95

"As a mother and as a citizen of a very wounded society, I am grateful to her for her voice and its capacity to heal us all."
— MARIANNE WILLIAMSON, author of *Illuminata*

Please ask for these titles at your book store, or to order directly, send payment (including $3.00 for the first book plus $1.00 for each additional book to cover shipping and handling fees) to: Crossroad, 370 Lexington Avenue, New York, NY 10017.

Also by Jon Mundy . . .

Awaken to Your Own Call
0-8245-1387-8 $11.95

"I have always felt that Jon Mundy does a wonderful job of explaining A *Course in Miracles*." — BEVERLY HUTCHINSON, Miracles Distribution Center

By Diane Berke . . .

Love Always Answers
0-8245-1432-7 $11.95

The Gentle Smile: Practicing Oneness in Daily Life
0-8245-1499-8 $13.95

"I celebrate Diane Berke's commitment to teaching higher truths. She is a light that illuminates my life." — DR. WAYNE DYER, author of *Everyday Wisdom*

Of related interest . . .

John Jacob Raub

Who Told You That You Were Naked?
0-8245-1203-0 $10.95

"A captivatingly simple conversation about a God who always loves and never punishes." — WILLIAM SHANNON, author of *Seeking the Face of God*

Ann Tremaine Linthorst

Mothering as a Spiritual Journey
0-8245-1250-0 $11.95

"As a mother and as a citizen of a very wounded society, I am grateful to her for her voice and its capacity to heal us all."
—MARIANNE WILLIAMSON, author of *Illuminata*

Please ask for these titles at your book store, or to order directly, send payment (including $3.00 for the first book plus $1.00 for each additional book to cover shipping and handling fees) to: Crossroad, 370 Lexington Avenue, New York, NY 10017.